CREDO PERSPECTIVES

VOLUMES ALREADY PUBLISHED

CREDO PERSPECTIVES

PLANNED AND EDITED BY
RUTH NANDA ANSHEN

MY SEARCH FOR ABSOLUTES

by PAUL TILLICH

with Drawings by

SAUL STEINBERG

A TOUCHSTONE BOOK
PUBLISHED BY SIMON AND SCHUSTER

SBN 671-20343-6
LIBRARY OF CONGRESS CATALOG CARD NUMBER: 67-16722
MANUFACTURED IN THE UNITED STATES OF AMERICA

2   3   4   5   6   7   8   9   10   11   12   13   14   15

To
Joan R. Brewster
     In Friendship
     and
     Gratitude

Contents

CREDO PERSPECTIVES

Their Meaning and Function

Credo Perspectives suggest that twentieth-century man is living in one of the world's most challenging periods, unprecedented in history, a dynamic period when he has almost unlimited choices for good and evil. In all civilizations of the world of our modern epoch, in both socialistic and capitalistic societies, we are faced with the compelling need to understand more clearly the forces that dominate our world and to modify our attitudes and behavior accordingly. And this will only happen if our best minds are persuaded and assembled to concentrate on the nature of this new epoch in evolutionary and moral history. For we are confronted with a very basic change. Man has intervened in the evolutionary process and he must better appreciate this fact with its influence on his life and work, and then try to develop the wisdom to direct the process, to recognize the mutable and the immutable elements in his moral nature and the relationship between freedom and order.

The authors in this series declare that science now per-
mits us to say that "objective" nature, the world which
alone is "real" to us as the one in which we all, scientists
included, are born, love, hate, work, reproduce and die,
is the world given us by our senses and our minds—a
world in which the sun crosses the sky from east to west,
a world of three-dimensional space, a world of values which
we, and we alone, must make. It is true that scientific
knowledge about macroscopic or subatomic events may
enable us to perform many acts we were unable to perform before. But it is as inhabitants of this human world
that we perform them and must finally recognize that there
is a certain kind of scientific "objectivity" that can lead us
to know everything but to understand nothing.

The symbol of *Credo Perspectives* is the Eye of Osiris.
It is the inner eye. Man sees in two ways: with his physical
eyes, in an empirical sensing or *seeing* by direct observation, and also by an indirect envisaging. He possesses in
addition to his two sensing eyes a single, image-making,
spiritual and intellectual Eye. And it is the *in-sight* of this
inner Eye that purifies and makes sacred our understanding
of the nature of things; for that which was shut fast has
been opened by the command of the inner Eye. And we
become aware that to believe is to see.

This series is designed to present a kind of intellectual
autobiography of each author, to portray the nature and
meaning of his creative process and to show the relevance
of his work to his feelings and aspirations. In it we hope
also to reflect the influence of the work on the man and
on society, and to point to the freedom, or lack of freedom,
to choose and pursue one profession rather than another.
For the creator in any realm must surrender himself to a
passionate pursuit of his labors, guided by deep personal
intimations of an as yet undiscovered reality.

Credo Perspectives hope to unlock a consciousness that at first sight may seem to be remote but is proved on acquaintance to be surprisingly immediate, since it stems from the need to reconcile the life of action with the life of contemplation, of practice with principle, of thought with feeling, of knowing with being. For the whole meaning of *self* lies within the observer, and its shadow is cast naturally on the object observed. The divorce of man from his work, the division of man into an eternal and temporal half, results in an estrangement of man from his creative source, and ultimately from his fellows and from himself.

The hope of this series is to suggest that the universe itself is a vast entity where man will be lost if it does not converge in the person; for material forces or energies, or impersonal ideals, or scientifically objectified learning are meaningless without their relevance for human life and their power to disclose, even in the dark tendencies of man's nature, a law transcending man's arbitrariness.

For the personal is a far higher category than the abstract universal. Personality itself is an emotional, not an intellectual, experience; and the greatest achievement of knowledge is to combine the personal within a larger unity, just as in the higher stages of development the parts that make up the whole acquire greater and greater independence and individuality within the context of the whole. Reality itself is the harmony which gives to the component particulars of a thing the equilibrium of the whole. And while physical observations are ordered with direct reference to the experimental conditions, we have in sensate experience to do with separate observations whose correlation can only be indicated by their belonging to the wholeness of mind.

It is the endeavor of the authors to show that man has reached a turning point in consciousness, that his relationship with his creativity demands a clarification that can widen and deepen his understanding of the nature of reality. Work is made for man, not man for work. This series hopes to demonstrate the sacramental character of work, which is more easily achieved when the principal objects of our attention have taken on a symbolic form that is generally recognized and accepted; and this suggests a *law* in the relationship of a person and his chosen discipline: that it is valuable only when the spiritual, the creative, life is strong enough to insist on some expression through symbols. For no work can be based on material, technological, historical, or physical aspirations alone.

The human race is now entering upon a new phase of evolutionary consciousness and progress, a phase in which, impelled by the forces of evolution itself, it must converge upon itself and convert itself into one single human organism infused by a reconciliation of knowing and being in their inner unity and destined to make a qualitative leap into a higher form of consciousness that would transcend and complement individual consciousness as we know it, or otherwise destroy itself. For the entire universe is one vast field, potential for incarnation and achieving incandescence here and there of reason and spirit. And in the whole world of *quality* with which by the nature of our minds we necessarily make contact, we here and there apprehend pre-eminent value. This can be achieved only if we recognize that we are unable to focus our attention on the particulars of a whole without diminishing our comprehension of the whole, and of course, conversely, we can focus on the whole only by diminishing our comprehension of the particulars which constitute the whole.

The kind of knowledge afforded by mathematical physics ever since the seventeenth century has come more and more to furnish mankind with an ideal for all knowledge.

This error about the nature of knowledge it is the hope of this series to expose. For knowledge is a process, not a product and the results of scientific investigation do not carry with them self-evident implications. There are now, however, signs of new centers of resistance among men everywhere in almost all realms of knowledge. Many share the conviction that a deep-seated moral and philosophical reform is needed concerning our understanding of the nature of man and the nature of knowledge in relation to the work man is performing, in relation to his *credo* and his life.

Credo Perspectives constitute an endeavor to alter the prevailing conceptions, not only of the nature of knowledge and work, but also of creative achievements in general, as well as of the human agent who inquires and creates, and of the entire fabric of the culture formed by such activities. In other words, this is an endeavor to show that what we see and what we do are no more and no less than what we are.

It is the endeavor of *Credo Perspectives* to define the new reality in which the estrangement of man from his work, resulting in the self-estrangement in man's existence, is overcome. This new reality is born through the reconciliation of what a man *knows* with what a man *is*. Being itself in all its presuppositions and implications can only be understood through the totality, through wholeness. St. Paul, who, like Isaiah before him, went into the marketplace not to secularize truth but to proclaim it, taught man that the "new creation" could be explained only by conquering the daemonic cleavages, the destructive split, in soul and cosmos. And that fragmentation always destroys a unity, produces a tearing away from the source and thereby creates disunity and isolation. The fruit can never be separated from the tree. The Tree of Life can never be disjoined from the Tree of Knowledge for both have *one and the same* root. And if man allows himself to fall into isolation, if he seeks to maintain a self segregated from the totality of which he is a necessary part, if he chooses to be unrelated to the original context of all created things in which he too has his place—including his own labors— then this act of apostasy bears fruit in the demiurgical presumption of *magic,* a form of animism in which man seeks an authority of the self, placing himself above the law of the universe by attempting to separate the inseparable. He thus creates an unreal world after having destroyed or deserted the real. And in this way the method of analysis, of scientific objectivity, which is good and necessary in its right place, is endowed with a destructive power when it is allowed to usurp a place for which it is not fitted.

The naturalist principle that man is the measure of all things has been shattered more than ever in our own age by the question, "What is the measure of man?" Postmodern man is more profoundly perplexed about the nature of man than his ancestors were. He is on the verge of spiritual and moral insanity. He does not know who he is. And having lost the sense of who and what he is, he fails to grasp the meaning of his fellow man, of his vocation and of the nature and purpose of knowledge itself. For what is not understood cannot be known. And it is this cognitive faculty which is frequently abrogated by the "scientific" theory of knowledge, a theory that refuses to recognize the existence of comprehensive entities as distinct from their particulars. The central act of knowing is indeed that form of comprehension which is never absent from any process of knowing and is finally its ultimate sanction.

Science itself acknowledges as real a host of entities that cannot be described completely in materialistic or mechanistic terms, and it is this transcendence out of the domain of science into a region from which science itself can be appraised that *Credo Perspectives* hope to define. For the essence of the ebb and flow of experience, of sensations, the richness of the immediacy of directly apprehended knowledge, the metaphysical substance of what assails our being, is the very act itself of sensation and affection and therefore must escape the net of rational analysis, yet is intimately related to every cognitive act. It is this increasing intellectual climate that is calling into birth once more the compelling Socratic questions, "What is the purpose of life, the meaning of work?" "What is man?" Plato himself could give us only an indirect answer: "Man is declared to be that creature who is constantly in search of himself, a creature who at every moment of his existence must examine and scrutinize the conditions of his existence. He is a being in search of meaning."

From this it is evident that there is present in the universe a *law* applicable to all nature including man and his work. Life itself then is seen to be a creative process elaborating and maintaining *order* out of the randomness of matter, endlessly generating new and unexpected structures and properties by building up associations that qualitatively transcend their constituent parts. This is not to diminish the importance of "scientific objectivity." It is, however, to say that the mind possesses a quality that cannot be isolated or known exclusively in the sense of objective knowledge. For it consists in that elusive humanity in us, our self, that knows. It is that inarticulate awareness that includes and *comprehends* all we know. It consists in the irreducible active voice of man and is recognized only in other things, only when the circle of consciousness closes around its universe of events.

Our hope is to point to a new dimension of morality—

not that of constraint and prohibition but a morality that
lies as a fountainhead within the human soul, a morality
of aspiration to spiritual experience. It suggests that necessity is laid upon us to infer entities that are not observed
and are not observable. For an unseen universe is necessary to explain the seen. The flux is seen, but to account
for its structure and its nature we infer particles of various
kinds to serve as the vertices of the changing patterns, placing less emphasis on the isolated units and more on the
structure and nature of relations. The process of knowing
involves an immaterial becoming, an immaterial identification, and finally, knowledge itself is seen to be a dependent
variable of immateriality. And somewhere along this spiritual pilgrimage man's pure observation is relinquished and
gives way to the deeper experience of awe, for there can be
no explanation of a phenomenon by searching for its origin
but only by discerning its immanent law—this quality of
transcendence that abides even in matter itself. The present
situation in the world and the vast accretion of knowledge
have produced a serious anxiety which may be overcome
by re-evaluating the character, kinship, logic and opera-
tion of man in relation to his work. For work implies goals
and intimately affects the person performing the work.
Therefore the correlation and relatedness of ideas, facts
and values that are in perpetual interplay could emerge
from these volumes as they point to the inner synthesis and
organic unity of man and his labors. For though no labor
alone can enrich the person, no enrichment can be achieved
without absorbing and intense labor. We then experience a
unity of faith, labor and grace which prepares the mind for
receiving a truth from sources over which it has no control.
This is especially true since the great challenge of our age
arises out of man's inventions in relation to his life.

Thus *Credo Perspectives* seek to encourage the perfection

not only of man's works but also and above all the ful-fillment of himself as a person. And so we now are summoned to consider not only man in the process of de-velopment as a human subject but also his influence on the object of his investigation and creation. Observation alone is interference. The naïve view that we can observe any system and predict its behavior without altering it by the very act of observation was an unjustified extrapola-tion from Newton's *Celestial Mechanics*. We can observe the moon or even a satellite and predict its behavior with-out perhaps appreciably interfering with it, but we cannot do this with an amoeba, far less with a man and still less with a society of men. It is the heart of the question of the nature of work itself. If we regard our labors as a process of shaping or forming, then the fruits of our labors play the part of a mold by which we ourselves are shaped. And this means, in the preservation of the identity of the knower and the known, that cognition and generation, that is, crea-tion, though in different spheres, are nevertheless alike.

It is hoped that the influence of such a series may help to overcome the serious separations between function and meaning and may show that the extraordinary crisis through which the world is passing can be fruitfully met by recognizing that knowledge has not been completely de-humanized and has not totally degenerated into a mere notebook overcrowded with formulas that few are able to understand or apply.

For mankind is now engaged in composing a new theme. Life never manifests itself in negative terms. And our hope lies in drawing from every category of work a conviction that nonmaterial values can be discovered in positive, af-firmative, visible things. The estrangement between the temporal and nontemporal man is coming to an end, com-munity is inviting communion, and a vision of the human condition more worthy of man is engendered, connecting ever more closely the creative mind with the currents of spiritual energy which breaks for us the bonds of habit and keeps us in touch with the permanence of being through our work.

And as, long ago, the Bearers of Bread were succeeded by the Bearers of Torches, so now, in the immediacies of life, it is the image of man and his vocation that can re-kindle the high passion of humanity in its quest for light. Refusing to divorce work from life or love from knowledge, it is action, it is passion that enhances our being.

We live in an expanding universe and also in the moral infinite of that other universe, the universe of man. And along the whole stretched arc of this universe we may see that extreme limit of complicity where reality seems to shape itself within the work man has chosen for his realization. Work then becomes not only a way of knowledge, it becomes even more a way of life—of life in its totality. For the last end of every maker is himself.

"And the places that have been desolate for ages shall be built in thee: thou shalt raise up the foundations of generation and generation; and thou shalt be called the repairer of the fences, turning the paths into rest."*

RUTH NANDA ANSHEN

---

* Isaiah, 58:12.

PROLOGUE

This volume in *Credo Perspectives* represents the last major thoughts of Professor Paul Johannes Tillich before his death in 1965.

In this credo, Tillich points to the absolute character of the moral imperative while recognizing at the same time its relative manifestation in every act man performs and in every decision he makes. Following the autobiographical material preceding the text itself, the reader confronts Professor Tillich's unique gift in depicting the structural indwelling and kinship between sensate experience and the logical nature of the mind, their seeming estrangement and yet their reconciliation. For man's burden and his greatness consist in the infinite obligation which is laid upon him and yet, paradoxically, his finite capacity to fulfill absolutely this obligation. Thus the search for ultimate meaning in the life, historical and spiritual, of each man persists not *because of* the existential contingencies of the human condition but *in spite of* them. In this process lies the ambiguous nature of reality, as well as of perfection, the final acceptance of which constitutes man's full maturity.

19

My Search for Absolutes presents the lectures given at the Chicago University Law School. Had Professor Tillich lived, he also intended to present them at Harvard University as the Noble Lectures. His death made this impossible. The vigor and extraordinary lucidity of Paul Tillich's mind and spirit shine throughout the text and inspire Saul Steinberg's remarkable drawings with the same power and insight. For both Tillich and Steinberg possess, each in his own unique manner, that charismatic power which is intimately related to man's deep need for order.

Steinberg's comprehension in depth of the questions of estrangement and reconciliation, the ambiguity of life, is reflected in his one-dimensional calligraphy and may be said to be the equivalent in art of the experience of insubstantiality, the de-identification of the modern spirit and mind which Tillich also mirrors in his search for absolutes. In what might be called a negative myth Steinberg *draws* attention to the phenomenon of contemporary existence. Steinberg, like a modern Kepler (though speaking through the medium of art rather than through the language of mathematics and cosmology), shows us that the highest parts of the universe, as of man's nature, are reserved for the habitation of substances more pure and more perfect than man in his merely historical and physical life can experience. Yet for this purity and this perfection, this absolute, man must inevitably and compellingly search, as Tillich's thesis also reveals. For even if man fails, as he usually does, his aspiration for the ultimate remains paradoxically unimpaired. Steinberg through his idiom in art, as Kepler through his idiom in cosmology, teaches us by means of symbolic lines, perpendiculars, ellipses, triangles, circles and squares, that it is impossible that there should be an infinite space superior to fixed stars since there is no such place in the world; and if there were, the star there situated would be imperceptible to us.

The greatness of Tillich, as of Steinberg, lies in the rejection on the part of both of a reality based upon the absurdity of an actually infinite distance between ourselves and a given star—whether this star is the Keplerian one or the ideal aspiration of Steinberg and Tillich. It is the objection in art as in theology against the possibility of an actually infinite creature. Both Tillich and Steinberg restrict themselves to the assertion that, just as in the series of numbers, so in world-extension, man can always go on without ever coming to an end, his nature aspiring to the infinite, to absolutes, yet limiting their actualization.

And Tillich, the contemporary Philo, affirms with Steinberg the need in man's nature and the demands of history for a reconciliation of the transcendent and the immanent. In this way both Tillich and Steinberg are united in the convergence of their minds, a convergence which they both experienced through an intellectual and spiritual empathy.

Now, after Tillich's death, the inclusion in *Credo Perspectives* of Tillich's *Search for Absolutes* and Steinberg's statement of his vision combine to demonstrate the yearnings and yet the restrictions which lie at the heart of man's quest. The discursive language of Tillich's philosophical theology wedded to the non-discursive language of Steinberg's art presents with eloquence and conviction the dual character of transcendence and actuality and is the answer to the question: Why is an artist invited to comment on a theologian?

Tillich, even as Philo before him, has recognized the relationship between Platonism, the Biblical tradition and the philosophical situation of our time. Tillich has rethought and re-examined the Biblical heritage in the light of the existential problems of our day. He has shown that the unity of empirical freedom and transcendent necessity characterizes all symbols, indicating the relation of the unconditional to the conditioned and thereby has represented for man in the twentieth century the synthesis of the historical and the contemporary spirit. The preamble of faith with which the philosophical theology of Tillich begins and ends, though no longer universally accepted unchallenged, has not completely disappeared. It still remains the preamble of the living philosophy of a great part of mankind in spite of apparent skepticism and despair.

The drawings of Steinberg, illustrating the beauty and relevance of the principle of complementarity restated in the language of art, bestow on Tillich's theology a further evidence of Tillich's metaphysical as well as his ethical and social teachings, based upon the same principles of the same preamble of faith, in spite of its ambiguity as experienced in the human predicament.

Thus a unique event has taken place in presenting Tillich and Steinberg within the same conceptual framework of reference; it demonstrates the convergence in depth, in two apparently divergent dimensions, of two of the most creative and seminal minds of this century.

In conclusion, gratitude is due to Paul Tillich's wife, Mrs. Hannah Tillich, for her generous cooperation in the preparation of this volume, as well as to Dr. Robert C. Kimball, the literary executor of Paul Tillich's estate. Dr. Kimball's devotion to Tillich, who was his teacher and mentor, prevailed throughout the preparation of the manuscript. And finally it should be affirmed that Mrs. Joan R. Brewster, to whom this volume is dedicated, has bestowed her devoted attention and efforts on the preparatory work.

RUTH NANDA ANSHEN

I

What Am I?

THE FACT THAT I WAS born on August 20, 1886, means that a part of my life belongs to the nineteenth century, especially if one assumes the nineteenth century to end (as one should) with August 1, 1914, the beginning of the First World War. Belonging to the nineteenth century implies life in relatively peaceful circumstances and recalls the highest flourishing of bourgeois society in its productive grandeur. It also implies aesthetic ugliness and spiritual disintegration. It implies, on the one hand, revolutionary impulses directed against this self-complacent period and, on the other hand, a consciousness of the Christian humanist values which underlie even the antireligious forms of this society and which made and make it possible to resist the

inhuman systems of the twentieth century. I am one
of those in my generation who, in spite of the radi-
calism with which they have criticized the nineteenth century, often feel a longing for its stability,
its liberalism, its unbroken cultural traditions.

My birthplace was a village with the Slavic name
Starzeddel, near Guben, a small industrial town in
the province of Brandenburg, at the Silesian border.
After four years my father, a minister of the Prussian Territorial Church, was called to the position
of superintendent of the diocese of Schönfliess-Neu-
mark. Superintendent was the title of the directing
minister in a group of parishes, with functions similar to those of a bishop but on a smaller scale.
Schönfliess was a place of three thousand inhabitants, in eastern Brandenburg. The town was medieval in character. Surrounded by a wall, built
around an old Gothic church, entered through gates
with towers over them, administered from a medieval town hall, it gave the impression of a small,
protected, and self-contained world. The environment was not much different when, from my twelfth
to fourteenth year, I stayed as a pupil of the humanistic Gymnasium, and as a boarder of two elderly
ladies, in Königsberg-Neumark, a town of seven
thousand people with the same kind of medieval
remains but bigger and more famous for their
Gothic perfection.

These early impressions may partly account for

what has been challenged as the romantic trend in my feeling and thinking. One side of this so-called romanticism is my relationship to nature. It is expressed in a predominantly aesthetic-meditative attitude toward nature as distinguished from a scientific-analytical or technical-controlling relation. It is the reason for the tremendous emotional impact that Schelling's philosophy of nature made upon me —although I was well aware that this philosophy was scientifically impossible. It is theologically formulated in my doctrine of the participation of nature in the process of fall and salvation. It was one of the reasons why I was always at odds with the Ritschlian theology which establishes an infinite gap between nature and personality and gives Jesus the function of liberating man's personal life from bondage to the nature within us and beside us. When I came to America I found that Calvinism and Puritanism were natural allies of Ritschlianism in this respect. Nature is something to be controlled morally and technically, and only subjective feelings of a more or less sentimental character toward nature are admitted. There is no mystical participation in nature, no understanding that nature is the finite expression of the infinite ground of all things, no vision of the divine-demonic conflict in nature.

When I ask myself about the biographical background of this so-called romantic relation to nature, I find three causes which probably worked together in the same direction. First, I find the actual communication with nature, daily in my early years, in my later years for several months of every year. Many memorable instances of "mystical participation" in nature recur in similar situations. A second cause of the romantic relation to nature is the impact of poetry. German poetic literature, even aside from the romantic school, is full of expressions of nature mysticism. There are verses of Goethe, Hölderlin, Novalis, Eichendorff, Nietzsche, George, and Rilke which never have ceased to move me as deeply as they did when I first heard them. A third cause of this attitude toward nature came out of my Lutheran background. Theologians know that one of the points of disagreement between the two wings of the Continental Reformation, the Lutheran and the Reformed, was the so-called "Extra Calvinisticum," the doctrine that the finite is not capable of the infinite (*non capax infiniti*) and that consequently in Christ the two natures, the divine and the human, remained outside each other. Against this doctrine the Lutherans asserted the "Infra Lutheranum"—namely, the view that the finite is capable of the infinite and consequently that in Christ there is a mutual in-dwelling of the two natures. This difference means that on Lutheran ground the vision of the presence of the infinite in everything finite is theologically affirmed, that nature mysticism is possible and real, whereas on

Calvinistic ground such an attitude is suspect of pantheism and the divine transcendence is understood in a way which for a Lutheran is suspect of deism.

Romanticism means not only a special relation to nature; it means also a special relation to history. To grow up in towns in which every stone is witness of a period many centuries past produces a feeling for history, not as a matter of knowledge but as a living reality in which the past participates in the present. I appreciated that distinction more fully when I came to America. In lectures, seminars, homes I visited, and personal conversation with American students I found that an immediate emotional identification with the reality of the past was lacking. Many of the students here had an excellent knowledge of historical facts, but these facts did not seem to concern them profoundly. They remained objects of their intellect and almost never became elements of their existence. It is the European destiny to experience in every generation the wealth and the tragedy of historical existence and consequently to think in terms of the past, whereas America's history started with the loss both of the burden and of the richness of the past. She was able to think in terms of the future. It is, however, not only historical consciousness generally which was emphasized by the romantic school; it was the special valuation of the European Middle

Ages through which romanticism was deeply influential in the intellectual history of the last one hundred years. Without this influence I certainly would not have conceived of the idea of theonomous periods in the past and of a new theonomy in the future.

Two other points of biographical significance ought to be mentioned in connection with the years in Schönfliess and Königsberg. The first is the effect which my early life in a parish house had upon me, standing as I did with a confessional Lutheran school on the one side and on the other a beautiful Gothic church in which Father was a successful pastor. It is the experience of the "holy" which was given to me at that time as an indestructible good and as the foundation of all my religious and theological work. When I first read Rudolf Otto's *Idea of the Holy* I understood it immediately in the light of these early experiences and took it into my thinking as a constitutive element. It determined my method in the philosophy of religion, wherein I started with the experiences of the holy and advanced to the idea of God and not the reverse way. Equally important existentially as well as theologically were the mystical, sacramental, and aesthetic implications of the idea of the holy, whereby the ethical and logical elements of religion were derived from the experience of the presence of the divine and not conversely. This made Schleiermacher congenial to me, as he was to Otto, and induced both Otto and myself to participate in movements for liturgical renewal and a revaluation of Christian and non-Christian mysticism.

Existence in a small town in eastern Germany before the turn of the century gave to a child with some imaginative power the feeling of narrowness and restrictedness. I have already referred to the surrounding wall as a symbol of this. Movement beyond the given horizon was restricted. Automobiles did not exist, and a secondary railway was built only after several years; a trip of a few miles was an event for man and beast alike. The yearly escape to the Baltic Sea, with its limitless horizon, was the great event, the flight into the open, into unrestricted space. That I had chosen, later, a place at the Atlantic Ocean for the days of my retirement is certainly due to those early experiences. Another form of escape from the narrowness of my early life came in making several trips to Berlin, the city in which my father was born and educated. The impression the big city made on me was somehow similar to that of the sea: infinity, openness, unrestricted space! But beyond this it was the dynamic character of life in Berlin that affected me, the immense amount of traffic, the masses of people, the ever-changing scenes, the inexhaustible possibilities. When, in the year 1900, my father was called to an important position in Berlin, I felt extreme joy. I never lost this feeling; in fact, it was deepened when I really learned of the "mysteries" of a world city and when I became able to participate in them. Therefore I always considered it a good destiny that the emigration of the year 1933 brought me to New York, the largest of all large cities.

Still deeper in their roots and their effects than restrictedness in space and movement were the sociological and psychological restrictions of those years. The structure of Prussian society before the First World War, especially in the eastern part of the kingdom, was authoritarian without being totalitarian. Lutheran paternalism made the father the undisputed head of the family, which included, in a minister's house, not only wife and children but also servants with various functions. The same spirit of discipline and authority dominated the public schools, which stood under the supervision of local and county clergy in their function as inspectors of schools. The administration was strictly bureaucratic, from the policeman in the street and the postal clerk behind the window, up through a hierarchy of officials, to the far-removed central authorities in Berlin—authorities as unapproachable as the "castle" in Kafka's novel. Each of these officials was strictly obedient to his superiors and strictly authoritative toward his subordinates and the public. What was still lacking in discipline was provided by the Army, which trespassed in power and social standing upon the civil world and drew the whole nation from earliest childhood into its ideology. It did this so effectively in my case that my enthusiasm for uniforms, parades, maneuvers, history of battles, and ideas of strategy was not exhausted until my thirtieth year, and then only because of my experiences in the First World War. But above all this, at the top of the hierarchy, stood the King of Prussia, who happened to be also the German Emperor. Patriotism involved, above all, adherence to the King and his house. The existence of a parliament, democratic forces, socialist movements, and of a strong criticism of the Emperor and the Army did not affect the conservative Lutheran groups of the East among whom I lived. All these democratic elements were rejected, distortedly represented, and characterized as revolutionary, which meant criminal. Again it required a world war and a political catastrophe before I was able to break through this system of authorities and to affirm belief in democratic ideals and the social revolution.

Most difficult to overcome was the impact of the authoritarian system on my personal life, especially on its religious and intellectual side. Both my father and mother were strong personalities. My father was a conscientious, very dignified, completely convinced and, in the presence of doubt, angry supporter of the conservative Lutheran point of view. My mother, coming from the more democratic and liberal Rhineland, did not have the authoritarian attitude. She was, however, deeply influenced by the rigid morals of Western Reformed Protestantism. The consequence was a restrictive pressure in thought as well as in action, in spite (and partly because) of a warm atmosphere of loving care. Every attempt to break through was prevented by the unavoidable guilt consciousness produced by identification of the parental with the divine authority. There was only one point at which resistance was possible—namely, by using the very principles established by my father's authoritarian system against this system itself. And this was the way I instinctively chose. In the tradition of classical orthodoxy, my father loved and used philosophy, convinced that there can be no conflict between a true philosophy and revealed truth. The long philosophical discussions which developed belong to the most happy instances of a positive relation to my father. Nevertheless, in these discussions the break-through occurred. From an independent philosophical position a state of independence spread out into all directions, theoretically first, practically later. It is this difficult and painful break-through to autonomy which has made me immune against any system of thought or life which demands the surrender of autonomy.

In an early polemic between Karl Barth and myself, he accused me of "still fighting against the

Grand Inquisitor." He is right in asserting that this is a decisive element of my theological thought. What I have called the "Protestant principle" is, as I believe, the main weapon against every system of heteronomy. But Karl Barth must have realized in the meantime that this fight never will become unnecessary. History has shown that the Grand Inquisitor is always ready to reappear in different disguises, political as well as theological. The fact that I have equally often been accused of neo-orthodoxy and of old liberalism is understandable in view of the two strong motives I received in the years under discussion: the romantic and the revolutionary motives. The balancing of these motives has remained the basic problem of my thought and of my life ever since.

In the year 1900 we moved to Berlin. I became a pupil at a humanistic Gymnasium in Old Berlin, passed my final examinations in 1904, and was matriculated in the theological faculties of Berlin, Tübingen, and Halle. In 1909 I took my first, in 1911 my second theological examination. In 1911 I acquired the degree of Doctor of Philosophy in Breslau and in 1912 the degree of Licentiat of Theology in Halle. In the latter year I received ordination into the Evangelical Lutheran Church of the province of Brandenburg. In 1914 I joined the German Army as a war chaplain. After the end of the war I became a Privatdozent of Theology at the

University of Berlin, the beginning of my academic
career. Reviewing these fifteen years of preparation,
interrupted and at the same time completed by the
war, I found abundant material for philosophical
reflection. But I must restrict myself to some observations about the impact of these years on my
own development.

In Königsberg, as well as in Berlin, I was a pupil
in a "humanistic Gymnasium." A Gymnasium, com-
pared with American institutions, consists of high
school plus two years of college. The normal age
for finishing the Gymnasium is eighteen. A humanist Gymnasium has as its central subjects Greek and
Latin. My love of the Greek language was a ve-
hicle for my love of Greek culture and especially the early Greek philosophers. One of my most
enthusiastically prepared and best received courses
had as its subject matter the pre-Socratic philosophy. The problem of the humanistic education is
its relation to the religious tradition which, even
without a special religious instruction, is omnipres-
ent in history, art, and literature. Whereas in the
United States the basic spiritual conflict is that between religion and scientific naturalism, in Europe
the religious and humanistic traditions (of which
the scientific world view is only a part) have been,
ever since the Renaissance, in continuous tension.
The German humanistic Gymnasium was one of the
places in which this tension was most manifest.

While we were introduced into classical antiquity in formal classes meeting about ten hours a week for about eight years, we encountered the Christian tradition at home, in the church, in directly religious instructions in school and outside the school, and in indirect religious information in history, literature, and philosophy. The result of this tension was either a decision against one side or the other, or a general skepticism or a split-consciousness which drove one to attempt to overcome the conflict constructively. The latter way, the way of synthesis, was my own way. It follows the classical German philosophers from Kant to Hegel and has remained a driving force in all my theological work. It has found its final form in my *Systematic Theology*.

Long before my matriculation as a student of theology I studied philosophy privately. When I entered the university I had a good knowledge of the history of philosophy and a basic acquaintance with Kant and Fichte. Schleiermacher, Hegel, and Schelling followed, and Schelling became the special subject of my study. Both my doctoral dissertation and my thesis for the degree of Licentiat of Theology dealt with Schelling's philosophy of religion. These studies seemed to foreshadow a philosopher rather than a theologian; and indeed they enabled me to become a professor of philosophy of religion and of social philosophy in the philosophical faculties of Dresden and Leipzig,

a professor of pure philosophy in Frankfurt, a lec-
turer in the philosophical departments of Columbia
and Yale, and a philosopher of history in connection with the religious-socialist movement. Nevertheless I was a theologian, because the existential
question of our ultimate concern and the existential
answer of the Christian message are and always
have been predominant in my spiritual life.

The fifteen years from 1904 to 1919 in various
ways contributed to this decision. My experiences
as a student of theology in Halle from 1905 to
1907 were quite different from those of theological
student Leverkuhn in Thomas Mann's *Doctor Faus-
tus* in the same period. There was a group of great
theologians to whom we listened and with whom we
wrestled intellectually in seminars and personal discussions. One thing we learned above all was that
Protestant theology is by no means obsolete but
that it can, without losing its Christian foundation,
incorporate strictly scientific methods, a critical
philosophy, a realistic understanding of men and
society, and powerful ethical principles and motives. Certainly we felt that much was left undone
by our teachers and had to be done by ourselves.
But this feeling of every new generation need not
obviate the gratefulness for what it has received
from its predecessors.

Important influences on our theological existence
came from other sides. One of them was our discov-

ery of Kierkegaard and the shaking impact of his dialectical psychology. It was a prelude to what happened in the 1920s when Kierkegaard became the saint of the theologians as well as of the philosophers. But it was only a prelude; for the spirit of the nineteenth century still prevailed, and we hoped that the great synthesis between Christianity and humanism could be achieved with the tools of German classical philosophy. Another prelude to the things to come occurred in the period between my student years and the beginning of the First World War. It was the encounter with Schelling's second period, especially with his so-called "Positive Philosophy." Here lies the philosophically decisive break with Hegel and the beginning of that movement which today is called Existentialism. I was ready for it when it appeared in full strength after the First World War, and I saw it in the light of that general revolt against Hegel's system of reconciliation which occurred in the decades after Hegel's death and which, through Kierkegaard, Marx, and Nietzsche, has become decisive for the destiny of the twentieth century.

But once more I must return to my student years. The academic life in Germany in these years was extremely individualistic. There were no dormitories for students and few, impersonal activities for the student body as such. The religious life was almost completely separated from the life of

the churches; chaplains for the students did not
exist and could hardly be imagined. The relation
with the professors and their families was sporadic
and in many cases completely absent. It is this situation which made the fraternities in Germany much
more important than they are in this country. My
membership in such a fraternity with Christian principles was not only a most happy but also a most
important experience. Only after the First World
War, when my eyes became opened to the political
and social scene, did I realize the tremendous dangers of our prewar academic privileges. And I
looked with great concern at the revival of the fraternities in post-Hitler Germany. But in my student
years the fraternity gave me a communion (the first
one after the family) in which friendship, spiritual
exchange on a very high level, intentional and unin-
tentional education, joy of living, seriousness about
the problems of communal life generally, and Christian communal life especially, could daily be experienced. I question whether without this experience I
would have understood the meaning of the church
existentially and theoretically.

The First World War was the end of my period
of preparation. Together with my whole generation
I was grasped by the overwhelming experience of a
nationwide community—the end of a merely individualistic and predominantly theoretical existence. I volunteered and was asked to serve as a war

chaplain, which I did from September 1914 to September 1918. The first weeks had not passed before my original enthusiasm disappeared; after a few months I became convinced that the war would last indefinitely and ruin all Europe. Above all, I saw that the unity of the first weeks was an illusion, that the nation was split into classes, and that the industrial masses considered the Church as an unquestioned ally of the ruling groups. This situation became more and more manifest toward the end of the war. It produced the revolution, in which imperial Germany collapsed. The way in which this situation produced the religious-socialist movement in Germany has often been described. I want, however, to add a few reflections. I was in sympathy with the social side of the revolution even before 1918, that side which soon was killed by the interference of the victors, by the weakness of the socialists and their need to use the Army against the communists; also by inflation and the return of all the reactionary powers in the middle of the Twenties. My sympathy for the social problems of the German revolution has roots in my early childhood which are hard to trace. Perhaps it was a drop of the blood which induced my grandmother to build barricades in the revolution of 1848, perhaps it was the deep impression upon me made by the words of the Hebrew prophets against injustice and by the words of Jesus against the rich; all these were words I learned by heart in my very early years. But whatever it was, it broke out ecstatically in those years and remained a continuing reality, although mixed with resignation and some bitterness about the division of the world into two all-powerful groups between which the remnants of a democratic and religious socialism are crushed. It was a mistake when the editor of the *Christian Century* gave to my article in the series "How My Mind Changed in the Last Ten Years" the title "Beyond Religious Socialism." If the prophetic message is true, there is nothing "beyond religious socialism."

Another remark must be made here regarding my relation to Karl Marx. It has always been dialectical, combining a Yes and a No. The Yes was based on the prophetic, humanistic, and realistic elements in Marx's passionate style and profound thought, the No on the calculating, materialistic, and resentful elements in Marx's analysis, polemics, and propaganda. If one makes Marx responsible for everything done by Stalin and the system for which he stands, an unambiguous No against Marx is the necessary consequence. If one considers the transformation of the social situation in many countries, the growth of a definite self-consciousness in the industrial masses, the awakening of a social conscience in the Christian churches, the universal application of the economic-social method of analysis to the history of thought—all this under the influence of Marx—then the No must be balanced by a Yes. Although today such a statement is unwelcome and even dangerous, I could not suppress it, as I could not suppress my Yes to Nietzsche during the time in which everything which deserves a No in him was used and abused by the Nazis. As long as our thought remains autonomous, our relation to the great historical figures must be a Yes and a No. The undialectical No is as primitive and unproductive as the undialectical Yes.

In the years after the revolution my life became more intensive as well as extensive. As a Privat-dozent of Theology at the University of Berlin (from 1919 to 1924), I lectured on subjects which included the relation of religion to politics, art, philosophy, depth psychology, and sociology. It was a "theology of culture" that I presented in my lectures on the philosophy of religion, its history and its structure. The situation during those years in Berlin was very favorable for such an enterprise. Political problems determined our whole existence; even after revolution and inflation they were matters of life and death. The social structure was in a state of dissolution; human relations with respect to authority, education, family, sex, friendship, and pleasure were in a creative chaos. Revolutionary art came into the foreground, supported by the Republic, attacked by the majority of the people. Psychoanalytic ideas spread and produced a consciousness of realities which had been carefully repressed in previous generations. Participation in these movements created manifold problems, conflicts, fears, expectations, ecstasies, and despairs, practically as well as theoretically. All this was at the same time material for an apologetic theology.

It was a benefit to me when, after almost five years in Berlin, my friendly adviser, the minister of education, Karl Becker, forced me against my desire into a theological professorship in Marburg. During the three semesters of my teaching there I encountered the first radical effects of neo-orthodox theology on theological students: Cultural problems were excluded from theological thought; theologians like Schleiermacher, Harnack, Troeltsch, Otto were contemptuously rejected; social and political ideas were banned from theological discussions. The contrast with my experiences in Berlin was overwhelming, at first depressing and then inciting: A new way had to be found. In Marburg, in 1925, I began work on my *Systematic Theology,* the first volume of which appeared in 1951. At the same time that Heidegger was in Marburg as professor of philosophy, influencing some of the best students, Existentialism in its twentieth-century form crossed my path. It took years before I became fully aware of the impact of this encounter on my own thinking. I resisted, I tried to learn, I accepted the new way of thinking more than the answers it gave.

In 1925 I was called to Dresden and shortly afterward to Leipzig also. I went to Dresden, declining a more traditional theological position in Giessen because of the openness of the big city both spatially and culturally. Dresden was a center of visual art, painting, architecture, dance, opera, with all of which I kept in close touch. The cultural situation was not much different when, in 1929, I received and accepted a call as professor of philosophy at the University of Frankfurt. Frankfurt was the most modern and most liberal university in Germany, but it had no theological faculty. So it was quite appropriate that my lectures moved on the boundary line between philosophy and theology and tried to make philosophy existential for the numerous students who were obliged to take philosophical classes. This, together with many public lectures and speeches throughout Germany, produced a conflict with the growing Nazi movement long before 1933. I was immediately dismissed after Hitler had become German Chancellor. At the end of 1933 I left Germany with my family and came to the United States.

In the years from 1919 to 1933 I produced all my German books and articles with the exception of a few early ones. The bulk of my literary work consists of essays, and three of my books—*Religiose Verwirklichung, The Interpretation of History,* and *The Protestant Era*—are collections of articles

which themselves are based on addresses or speeches.
This is not accidental. I spoke or wrote when I was
asked to do so, and one is more often asked to write
articles than books. But there was another reason:
Speeches and essays can be like screws, drilling into
untouched rocks; they try to take a step ahead, perhaps successfully, perhaps in vain. My attempts to
relate all cultural realms to the religious center had
to use this method. It provided new discoveries—
new at least for me—and, as the reaction showed,
not completely familiar to others. Essays like those
on "The Idea of a Theology of Culture," "The Over-
coming of the Concept of Religion in the Philosophy
of Religion," "The Demonic," "The Kairos," "Be-
lief-ful Realism," "The Protestant Principle and the
Proletarian Situation," "The Formative Power of
Protestantism" and, in America, "The End of the
Protestant Era," "Existential Philosophy," "Religion
and Secular Culture" and my books *Dynamics of
Faith* and *Morality and Beyond*—these were decisive
steps on my cognitive road. So were the Terry Lectures which I delivered at Yale in October 1950
under the title "The Courage to Be." This method
of work has the advantages referred to, but it also
has its shortcomings. There is even in a well-
organized work such as my *Systematic Theology* a
certain inconsistency and indefiniteness of terminology; there is the influence of different, sometimes
competitive motives of thought, and there is a tak-

ing for granted of concepts and arguments which have been dealt with in other places.

The first volume of *Systematic Theology* is dedicated "to my students here and abroad." *The Protestant Era* could have been dedicated "to my listeners here and abroad"—that is, to the numerous nonstudent audiences to whom I spoke in addresses, speeches, and sermons. Looking back at more than forty years of public speaking, I must confess that from the first to the last address this activity gave me the greatest anxiety and the greatest happiness. I have always walked up to a desk or pulpit with fear and trembling, but the contact with the audience gave me a pervasive sense of joy, the joy of a creative communion, of giving and taking, even if the audience was not vocal. But when it became vocal, in periods of questions or discussions, this exchange was for me the most inspiring part of the occasion. Question and answer, Yes and No in an actual disputation—this original form af all dialectics is the most adequate form of my own thinking. But it has a deeper implication. The spoken word is effective not only through the meaning of the sentences formulated but also through the immediate impact of the personality behind these sentences. This is a temptation because one can use it for methods of mere persuasion. But it is also a benefit, because it agrees with what may be called "existential truth"—namely, a truth which lives in the immediate self-

expression of an experience. This is not true of
statements which have a merely objective character,
which belong to the realm of "controlling knowledge," but it is valid of statements which concern
us in our very existence and especially of theological
statements which deal with that which concerns us
ultimately. To write a system of existential truth,
therefore, is the most difficult task confronting a
systematic theologian. But it is a task which must be
tried again in every generation, in spite of the danger that either the existential element destroys systematic consistency or that the systematic element
suffocates the existential life of the system.

To begin life anew in the United States at forty-
seven years of age and without even a minimum
knowledge of the language was rather difficult.
Without the help of colleagues and students at
Union Theological Seminary and the assistance of
German and American friends it might easily have
been disastrous. It was for over eighteen years that I
taught at the Seminary, and after my retirement age
I continued my bonds of friendship with Union
Seminary.

It was first of all a shelter at the moment when
my work and my existence in Germany had come to
an end. The fact that shortly after my dismissal by
Hitler I was asked by Reinhold Niebuhr (who happened to be in Germany that summer) to come to
Union Seminary prevented me from becoming a

refugee in the technical sense. Our family arrived in New York on November 4, 1933. At the pier we were received by Professor Horace Friess of the philosophy department of Columbia University, who had asked me in Germany to give a lecture in his department. Ever since 1933 I had been in close relation to the Columbia philosophers, and the dialectical conversation across Broadway (the street separating Columbia and Union) never ceased but rather developed into an intensive cooperation. It was Union, however, that took me in as a stranger, then as visiting, associate, and full professor. Union Seminary was not only a shelter in the sense of affording a community of life and work. The Seminary is a closely knit community of professors and their families, of students, often likewise with their families, and of the staff. The members of this fellowship meet one another frequently in elevators and halls, at lectures, in religious services and social gatherings. The problems as well as the blessings of such a community are obvious. For our introduction into American life all this was invaluable, and it was also important for me as a counteraction against the extreme individualism of one's academic existence in Germany.

Union Seminary, moreover, is not an isolated community. If New York is the bridge between the continents, Union Seminary is the lane of that bridge, on which the churches of the world move. A

continuous stream of visitors from all countries and
all races passed through our quadrangle. It was almost impossible to remain provincial in such a setting. Union's world-wide outlook theologically, culturally, and politically was one of the things for
which I was most grateful. The cooperation of the
faculty had been perfect. During eighteen years at
Union Seminary I had not had a single disagreeable
experience with my American colleagues. I regret
only that the tremendous burden of work prevented
us from enjoying a more regular and more extensive
exchange of theological ideas. The work at the Seminary was first of all a work with students. They
came from all over the continent, including Canada.
They were carefully selected, and their number was
increased by exchange students from all over the
world. I loved them from the first day because of
their human attitude toward everything human (including myself); because of their openness to ideas,
even if strange to them, as my ideas certainly were;
because of their seriousness in study and self-educa-
tion in spite of the confusing situation in which they
found themselves in a place like Union Seminary.
The lack of linguistic and historical preparation
produced some difficulties, but these were overbal-
anced by many positive qualities. Union Seminary
is not only a bridge between the continents but also
a center of American life. Its faculty, therefore, is
drawn into innumerable activities in New York and

in the rest of the country, and the more so the longer one is on the faculty. It is obvious that in spite of the great benefits one can derive from such contacts with the life of a whole continent, the scholarly work is reduced in time and efficiency.

Beyond all this, Union Seminary gives to its members a place of common worship. This was a new experience for me, and a very significant one. It provided for the faculty an opportunity to relate theological thought to their own, and to the general, devotional life of the Church. It created for the students the possibility of experiencing this relation of thought to life and thereby of judging the one in the light of the other. It placed upon me the obligation of expressing myself in meditations and in sermons as well as in the abstract theological concepts of lectures and essays. This added in a profound way to the thanks I owe to Union Theological Seminary.

For external and practical reasons it became impossible to maintain the relationship to artists, poets, and writers which I enjoyed in postwar Germany. But I have been in permanent contact with the depth-psychology movement and with many of its representatives, especially in the last ten years. The problem of the relation between the theological and the psychotherapeutic understanding of men has come more and more into the foreground of my interest partly through a university seminar on religion and health at Columbia University, partly through

the great practical and theoretical interest that depth
psychology aroused in Union Seminary, and partly
through personal friendship with older and younger
analysts and counselors. I do not think that it is possible today to elaborate a Christian doctrine of man,
and especially a Christian doctrine of the Christian
man, without using the immense material brought
forth by depth psychology.

The political interests of my postwar years in
Germany remained alive in America. They found
expression in my participation in the religious-
socialist movement in this country; in the active relationship I maintained for years with the Graduate
Faculty of Political Science at the New School for
Social Research, New York; in my chairmanship of
the Council for a Democratic Germany during the
war; and in the many religio-political addresses I
gave. In spite of some unavoidable disappointments,
especially with the Council, politics remained, and
always will remain, an important factor in my theological and philosophical thought. After the Second
World War, I felt the tragic more than the activating
elements of our historical existences, and I lost the
inspiration for, and the contact with, active politics.

Emigration at the age of forty-seven means that
one belongs to two worlds: to the Old as well as to
the New into which one has been fully received. The
connection with the Old World had been maintained in different ways: first of all through a con-

tinuous community with the friends who had left Germany as refugees like myself, whose help, criticism, encouragement, and unchanging friendship made everything easier and yet one thing—namely, the adaptation to the New World—more difficult. But it was my conviction, confirmed by many American friends, that a too quick adaptation is not what the New World expects from the immigrant but rather the preservation of the old values and their translation into the terminology of the new culture. Another way of keeping contact with the Old World was the fact that for more than fifteen years I had been the chairman of the Self-help for Emigrés from Central Europe, an organization of refugees for refugees, giving advice and help to thousands of newcomers every year, most of them Jews. This activity brought me into contact with many people from the Old World whom I never would have met otherwise, and it opened to view depths of human anxiety and misery and heights of human courage and devotion which are ordinarily hidden from us. At the same time it revealed to me aspects of the average existence in this country from which I was far removed by my academic existence.

A third contact with the Old World was provided by my political activity in connection with the Council for a Democratic Germany. Long before the East-West split became a world-wide reality, it was visible in the Council and with many tragic consequences. The present political situation in Germany—as distinguished from the spiritual situation—lost nothing of this character. I saw it as thoroughly tragic, a situation in which the element of freedom is as deeply at work as is the element of fate, which is the case in every genuine tragedy. This impression was fully confirmed by my two trips to Germany after the Second World War. I lectured at several German universities, in 1948 mainly at Marburg and Frankfurt, in 1951 mainly at the Free University in Berlin. Of the many impressions these visits gave me, I want to point only to the spiritual situation in Germany, which was open, surprisingly open, for the ideas which are discussed in this volume. An evidence of this was the speed with which my English writings were translated and published in Germany. This way of returning to Germany is the best I could imagine, and it made me very happy.

But in spite of these permanent contacts with the Old World, the New World grasped me with its irresistible power of assimilation and creative courage. There is no authoritarian system in the family —as my two children taught me, sometimes through tough lessons. There is no authoritarian system in the school—as my students taught me, sometimes through amusing lessons. There is no authoritarian system in the administration—as the policemen taught me, sometimes through benevolent lessons.

There is no authoritarian system in politics—as the elections taught me, sometimes through surprise lessons. There is no authoritarian system in religion—as the denominations taught me, sometimes through the presence of a dozen churches in one village. The fight against the Grand Inquisitor could lapse, at least this was so before the beginning of the second half of this century.

But beyond this I saw the American courage to go ahead, to try, to risk failures, to begin again after defeat, to lead an experimental life both in knowledge and in action, to be open toward the future, to participate in the creative process of nature and history. I also saw the dangers of this courage, old and new ones, and I confess that some of the new ones began to give me serious concern. Finally, I saw the point at which elements of anxiety entered this courage and at which the existential problems made an inroad among the younger generation in this country. Although this situation constitutes one of the new dangers, it also means openness for the fundamental question of human existence: "What am I?" the question that theology and philosophy both try to answer.

Looking back at a long life of theological and philosophical thought, I ask myself how it can compare with the world of our predecessors in the last generations. Neither I myself nor anybody else can answer this question today. One thing, however, is

evident to most of us in my generation: We are not
scholars according to the pattern of our teachers at
the end of the nineteenth century. We were forced
into history in a way which made the analysis of history and of its contents most difficult. Perhaps we
have had the advantage of being closer to reality
than they were. Perhaps this is only a rationalization
of our shortcomings. However this may be, my work
has come to its end.

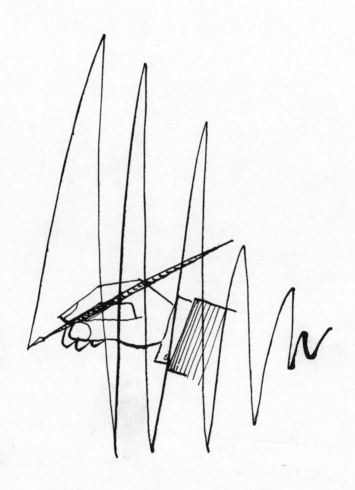

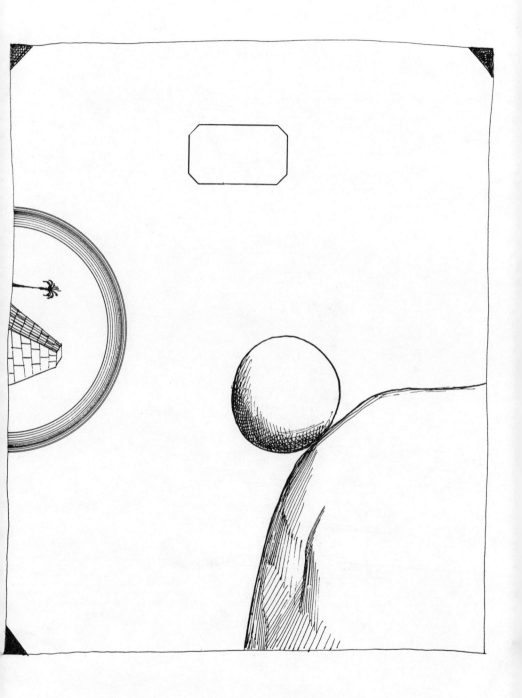

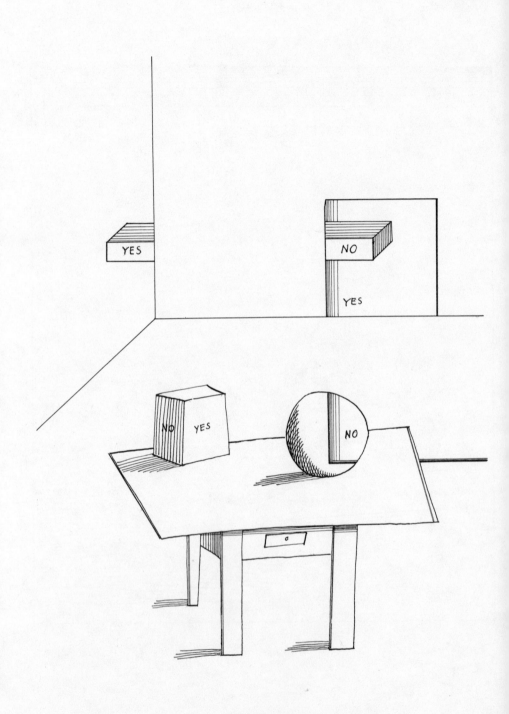

II

Absolutes in Human Knowledge and the Idea of Truth

MY CHOICE OF THIS SUBJECT was made out of a feeling of uneasiness—uneasiness about the victory of relativism in all realms of thought and life today. When we look around us, this seems to be a total victory. There is the great spectacle of scientific relativism, observable not only in the preliminary character of every scientific statement but also in the *model* aspect of scientific constructs and in the fact that terms like "atoms," "molecules," "energy," and "movement" are on a boundary line between model and concept. This gives a relativistic character even to scientific thinking. If you ask which model or concept is closest to reality you may receive the answer: none is; what we have here is a "game."

There is also the positivistic and formalistic character of much contemporary philosophy, which leaves the answers to problems of human existence —problems of "to be, or not to be"—to tradition, to arbitrary decisions and, in reaction against this, to despotism.

There is the growth of ethical relativism in theory and in practice.

Finally, there is a great and increasing relativism in the most sacred and perhaps most problematic of all realms, that of religion. It is visible today in the encounter of religions all over the world and in the secularist criticism of religion.

However, there are people, and I am among them, who are unwilling to accept this description and to surrender to an absolute relativism, not because we are authoritarian or reactionary but for definite reasons both theoretical and pragmatic.

The logical position against any claim of relativism to absoluteness is that "absolute relativism" is a self-contradictory term, an impossible combination of words. If one avoids this impossible combination of words, relativism itself becomes relative; therefore an element of absoluteness is not only a possibility but even a necessity, otherwise no assertion at all can be made.

But absolute relativism is also impossible practically. If I am asked to surrender totally to relativism I can say, "But I live! I know what 'true' and 'false' mean, I do something I can describe as 'better' than something else, I venerate something which concerns me ultimately and which for me is holy." The question then is: How can one make such statements if relativism has the last word? In the different realms of man's encounter with reality there must be some absolutes that make meaningful life possible, or it would be like the chaos before creation, described in Genesis. Therefore I believe it may be a service to life itself to find these absolutes and to show their validity and their limits.

Subject and Object

I shall begin my search for absolutes by looking for them in the most abstract and difficult but theoretically fundamental realm—the cognitive—the realm of knowing. What does "absolute" mean here?

Absolute (from the Latin *absolvere,* "to loosen,") means detached or freed from any limiting relation, from any particular relation, and even from the basis of all particular relations, the relation of subject and object. The term "absolute" has become difficult to use because many people associate it with the image of "an absolute thing" often identified with God. This, of course, is not what I mean. Therefore it is useful to explain the meaning of absolutes with the help of other terms, pairs of terms like "the unconditional and the conditioned," "the ultimate and the preliminary," "the infinite and the finite." I prefer to use the term "ultimate" in a phrase like "ultimate concern," the term "unconditional" in reference to the unconditional character of the ethical imperative, whatever its contents may be, and the term "infinite" in the religious realm. All these terms point to one thing: There is something that resists the stream of relativities.

The question is: Does the idea of truth presuppose something absolute and unconditional, and, if it does, can this absolute be found in the processes of knowing? Is everything in human knowledge relative, or is there an absolute in human knowledge?—although I should like to emphasize that there is no such thing as absolute knowledge, an impossibility.

Knowledge is based on an original unity and involves a separation and a reunion of subject and object. In this respect knowledge is like love, as the late Greek thinkers knew. The Greek word *gnosis,* "knowledge," had three meanings: sexual love, the knowledge of essences, and mystical union with the divine. Both knowledge and love are forms of union of the separated who belong to each other and want to reunite. In both cases we have original unity, necessary separation, and possible reunion.

This shows the ambiguity of the subject-object structure of the human mind, something we all have and know and experience in almost every moment. A structure that makes it possible for me as subject to look at you as object and even at myself as object is necessary in order to have truth as actual reality. It is necessary for the existence of truth. On the other hand, it is problematic because in every moment in which we reach truth we have overcome in some way this split between subject and object. So the question of the absolute in knowledge is identical with the question: How is the unavoidable split between subject and object overcome in the act of knowing?

There are three situations in which subject and object are united. The first is the material unity of subject and object in every sense impression. For instance, let us say that I am seeing a certain color —red. This experience cannot be denied even if it is a dream or a hallucination. Its cause is open to doubt, but the experience itself, an experience of redness as such, is immediate and certain. What I see is not my object any longer. It is in me and I am in it. The split is overcome and the complete reality is a mutual being in each other. This is the first example of something absolute in cognition. It is an immediate knowledge that has the character of absoluteness.

A second example in which the separation of subject and object is overcome is not material but formal. It is the logical and semantic structure of the mind, present always in every sense impression as well as in descriptions and explanations of the contents of a sense impression, and presupposed in every methodologically disciplined language. This logical and semantic structure is the other absolute in our experience, but again, to avoid confusion, let us observe that it is not a logical or semantic theory which is absolute. There are many such theories. What is absolute is the underlying structure that makes any theory about it possible. Whoever gives a new theory of logic or semantics uses logic or semantics in order to do this. He presupposes that about which he wants to give a theory. It is the structure of the mind that enables any theory, even one about the structure of the mind, to do what it attempts to do. This same absolute is presupposed in every argument for relativism. He who speaks for relativism presupposes the validity of logic in argument; therefore the consistent relativist cannot argue but can only shake his head.

Sense impressions and logical structure point to an even more fundamental absolute—the certainty even a relativistic philosopher has of himself as a relativistic philosopher. This is the old argument against radical skepticism formulated by Augustine, Descartes, and many others. Within our context itself the teacher of relativism has no doubt of himself as teacher of relativism. Here he is caught against his will by something absolute that embraces both the absoluteness of sense impressions and the absoluteness of logical form.

All this shows that the very concept of knowledge

presupposes an absolute structure within the flux of relative knowledge. The human mind could not maintain its centeredness, its self-awareness, without something that remains absolute in the stream of changing relativities. Every act of knowledge confirms this powerful safeguard against getting lost in that stream.

One of the most revealing absolutes in the process of thinking is the power to ask questions. I suggest that you sit down some day and do nothing but sit and think—not even read anything—just think, perhaps for as long as a whole hour, of what it means that there are beings called "men," who are able to ask questions. In this simple phenomenon a whole world is implied and a demonstration is given of the interdependence of subject and object in every cognitive approach. The asking subject in every question already has something of the object about which he asks, otherwise he could not ask. But he remains separated from the object of his thought and strives for union with it, which means for truth. Having and not having is the nature of questions, and everyone who asks confirms this interdependent subject-object structure of the mind as an absolute for men as men.

The Absoluteness of Essences

Until now we have found absolutes in experience. Are there absolutes in the reality that is experienced? There are.

Three groups of components are always met with in every encountered reality: essences, ontological structures, and being-itself. If you imagine an encounter with "redness," for instance, you can say that in this experience there are two quite different components. In it we encounter beings (things that are red), and we encounter qualities of beings (their redness).

Beings—for instance human beings (or desks or walls or trees)—are immersed in the stream of relativities. They come and go. They change, remain hidden, appear and disappear again. They *are*. But their being is becoming, and their becoming is a process of mutual encounters. We encounter people, including ourselves. We encounter other living beings and things. All of these encounter us and each other. Everything encounters everything else, directly, as a part of its environment, indirectly, as a part of the world. In these encounters being is manifest as becoming.

There is a fascination in this view of being as becoming for many of our contemporaries—philosophers, poets, all kinds of thinking human beings. It is this fascination which contributes most to the victory of relativism in our times. If we look at ourselves, however, and analyze the fascination, we discover that it is possible only because we are not just within the movement of being as becoming but above it. We can look at it, we know of it, we like it or are afraid of it, and this power of knowing is an absolute which makes it possible for us both to recognize and to be fascinated by the relative.

There are several absolutes in the stream of these relative encounters. The first is the absolute that makes language possible. The second is the absolute that makes understanding possible. And the third is the absolute that makes truth possible.

Man has language that denotes. This is one side of language. The other side is communication, which can be achieved in sounds by animals as well as by men; but denotative language presupposes a power possessed only by man among the beings we know. This power is the power of abstraction, the power to create universals in terms of language.

Think again about the experience of seeing a color, an experience in which subject and object are not separated. One is in the situation of seeing this red object, but there is something more here. This is only one side of what one perceives. The other side is red perceived as red wherever it appears. What one sees when one sees the red object close to is also *redness*—that is, in the particular red object the universal "redness" appears. To recognize this is to have the power of abstraction. The word "abstraction" is not highly honored today; therefore some people prefer a word like "ideation," but I prefer to give back to "abstraction" the honor it should have.

One perceives mentally the essence "red" in every red object (our word "essence" being what Plato called *eidos,* or Idea.) "Redness" is universally present in every red object, and we experience the word "red" as created with this perception, a perception of the essence "redness." "Redness" as an essence is not a thing beside other things. It is the transtemporal potentiality of all red things in the universe. It is absolute in the sense of independent of any particular moment in which "redness" appears and even of a situation in which cosmic events could produce its complete disappearance. Changes in the universe may make the appearance of "redness" impossible someday, but once upon a time it appeared, and the essence "redness" is beyond these possible changes. (Think of the appearance of men on the earth. It was impossible for a long time, for perhaps billions of years, but eventually what we know as "man" became actual. However, man never could have appeared if the essence "man" had not belonged to the potentialities of being.) It is the power of abstraction that makes us able to recognize "redness" in all red objects, to choose to buy something red instead of something green, and vice versa; that is, abstraction liberates us from bondage to the particular by giving us the power to create universals.

We find another type of essences in species and genera. In every pine tree we experience, first, this particular tree in our back yard, second, the species "pine" which enables us to produce a word "pine" and to plant a pine tree instead of an oak tree, and third, the genus "tree" which gives us this word and enables us to grow a tree instead of a shrub (and we could go on to speak of a plant and of an organic being and decide against having a sculpture in our garden).

Abstraction gives us the power of language, language gives us freedom of choice, and freedom of choice gives us the possibility of infinite technical production. It is interesting that in the symbolic story of the Paradise, as told in Genesis, language (the naming of animals and plants) is combined with technical activity (the cultivation of the garden). All this would be impossible without the absolutes we call "essences," through which language can come into existence.

Now I want to ask a question with far-reaching implications. Are there essences for individual human beings? Certainly there is a universal essence "man," usually referred to as "human nature," which makes it possible for us to have this word "man" and to recognize men as men. But is there beyond this an essence for Socrates, and for Augustine, and for you, and for me, something independent of our temporal becoming?

There is a tradition in philosophy that denies such an essence—the Aristotelian—and another that affirms it—the Neo-Platonic-Augustinian. I can give a pragmatic argument in support of the affirmative view, because it happens that there is a special category of people who acknowledge an essence for the individual, something absolute in him. They don't always do this philosophically, but they do it through their works. They are the artists who create essential images of individuals in paint or stone, in drama or novel, in poetry or biography. They try to show the absolute, essential man, who shines through the temporal manifestations of a human being.

Individual essences of men are also expressed in personal names, and personal names themselves are astonishing things. In religious myths one sees how the meaning of names was recognized. In Biblical language, God calls us by name, or our names are written in the book of life. On the opposite side, demons have names and it is the work of the Savior to recognize them and thus deprive the demons of their power. There are fairy tales in which someone tries to keep a name secret, because disclosing it would reveal something essential, transtemporal. These are all expressions of "individual essence," or of the individual's essence as absolute over against his changing temporal existence. And of course this has bearing on the symbolism of eternity and eternal life. It sets a definite limit to the dominance of the category of becoming.

The Absoluteness of Structures of Being

There is a second group of absolutes in man's cognitive encounters with reality—the structures of

being, which make the world of becoming possible
as a world. "World" means a unity in infinite mani-
foldness, a universe, a cosmos. (*Kosmos* is a Greek
word meaning both "world" and "harmony," or
centered unity.)

As the power of abstraction leads to the discovery
of the essences in our encounter with reality, and
from them to universals and their expression in human language, so the power of questioning the encounter with reality leads to discovery of the
universal structures of being, in which the whole of
relativities moves. The search for these structures is
an everlasting task.

Certain groups of them have been called "categories"—for example, causality and substance, quality and quantity.

Others have been called "forms of perception"—
for example, time and space.

There are those called "polarities" (a solvent
word)—for example, individualization and participation, dynamics and form, freedom and destiny.

And there are those that could be called "states
of being," such as essence and existence, finite and
infinite.

Others were called, in the Middle Ages, "*transcendentalia*": the good and the true and being-itself.

These are infinite problems of philosophy, and
we cannot go into them here; we can only relate
them to our central problem. Absolutes within the

relativities of encountered reality, they all appear continually, in the thought of skeptics as well as absolutists, in the thought of relativists as well as absolutists, of pluralists as well as monists. They appear in the most ordinary talk of daily life as well as in literature and philosophy, and they appear even in the most antimetaphysical philosophy. We live in the structures they give us. They provide us with the ontological safety without which neither thinking nor acting would be possible.

Imagine what would happen if, without anyone turning these pages, they turned themselves! Our whole world would break down in this moment, because the category of causality had disappeared; and the shock of this would be as great to the skeptic as to the dogmatist.

We could take another example—the category of substance. A complete loss of our identity would follow its disappearance. We can see an imagined occurrence of this in Kafka's novella of the metamorphosis of a man into a cockroach. The horrifying character of this story shows how deeply we are bound to the category of substance, which guarantees our identity.

These basic structures make possible our excursions of thought into the unsafe flux and relativity of encountered things. They give us the structure of thought as well as the structure of reality.

But now I must allow the relativist a word. He

rightly points to the fact that although time is a condition of our finite existence, the character of time is differently understood from Aristotle to Einstein, and although causality is implied in every explanation, the interpretations of causality and the distinction of different types of causality are always changing. He knows that even if every peasant woman who has never heard the word "substance" uses this category when she distinguishes herself as an individual from her husband, struggles are still going on between philosophers and theologians, in the West and in the East, about the meaning of the category of substance. And this is what the relativist has to say.

In answer to his criticism of these absolutes, I admit that our group of categories and our knowledge-grasp of the character of categories are relative. However, I still have to say that in the struggle about the meaning of categories they are always effective, whatever they mean and whatever philosophers say that they mean. Without their directing presence no struggle about their meaning would be possible. Their fundamental structural presence is therefore independent of any attempt to describe them and to understand their meaning.

If the relativist's argument against absolutes in the cognitive encounter with reality turns to the polarities and invalidates them by denying one pole, thus undercutting the other pole also, it is not difficult to show again how solidly even this relativist is rooted in the structures whose basic character he denies.

Take, for example, an important pair of polarities—freedom and destiny. The relativist may call them nonsense, or say that they are unnecessary for the cognitive process, or he may reject them as metaphysical imaginings.

Suppose that he does this. Now life suddenly puts him in the next moment before a decision, perhaps a theoretical decision, perhaps a practical one. After serious deliberation he decides. He does not feel that he was forced into it by external threats or by internal compulsions, nor does he feel that he decided arbitrarily. He was free, neither dependent on destiny alone nor on freedom alone, in his decision. It came out of the uniting center of his whole being, within which and centered by it was the whole of his life experiences, the whole of the movements within his body up to the moment of his decision, his destiny that he is this individual and no other.

He cannot escape these considerations. He denies the polarity of freedom and destiny, but when he had to make a decision—perhaps just about some theory of freedom—he was moving between the two poles.

If, in order to escape having to admit this, he denies one of the poles—for instance, the pole of freedom—he has ceased to be a relativist and has become a dogmatic adherent of determinism. But then his decision for determinism is itself determined, is merely a matter of his destiny, has no truth value and should claim none, for he had no alternative.

Such a discussion shows the polarities as absolutes in the relativities of the cognitive encounter with reality.

Summing up, we can say: Each of our statements about the absolutes in knowledge is relative, and this is true of my own statements here and now. But the absolutes themselves are not relative. One cannot escape them. Even if I had argued against them, I'd have had to use them to do so.

The Absoluteness of Being-Itself

We have discussed the absoluteness of the essences that make language possible and the absoluteness of the structures of being that make understanding possible. Now we have come to the absolute that underlies all the other absolutes as well as the stream of relativities, the absolute that makes the idea of truth possible. This absolute is being-itself.

You can deny every statement, but you cannot deny that being *is*. And if you ask what this "is" means, you arrive at the statement that it is the negation of possible non-being. "Is" means "is not

not." One cannot imagine non-being; one can only experience its threat. Therefore philosophy can say metaphysically, and with good logic support, that being is the power of resisting non-being. This is the most fundamental of all absolutes. You can deny anything particular whatsoever, but not being, because even your negative judgments themselves are acts of being and are only possible through being. Being is the basic absolute.

Let us listen again to the relativist. He says that this statement is as true as it is empty. The term "being" may be the basic one in all thought because thought is directed toward what *is,* but "being-itself" is just an abstraction covering everything that is. This means that one has in it only a completely empty absolute; and this, perhaps, a relativist is willing to concede. But the question is: *Is* "being-itself" an empty absolute?

There are two concepts of being. One is the result of the most radical abstraction and means not being this, not being that, not being anything particular, simply *being.* This indeed is an empty absolute.

The other concept of being is the result of two profound experiences, one of them negative, the other positive. The negative experience is the shock of non-being that can be experienced in theoretical imagination by those who are philosophers by nature. If one is not a philosopher, one can have it as a simple human being, in the practical experience of having to die.

But there is not only the shock of non-being. There is also a positive experience. It is the experience of *eros*—"love" in Greek—the love of being as such, a mystical relation to being-itself. This is what Augustine called *"amor amoris"* ("love of love") and Spinoza called *"amor intellectualis"* ("intellectual love"). One could also call it a feeling for the holiness of being as being, whatever it may be. This "being" transcends everything particular without becoming empty, for it embraces everything particular. "Being" in this sense is power of being, and it is an infinitely full, inexhaustible but indefinite absolute. It is the basis of truth, because it is the transcendance of subject and object. It is the basis of the good, because it contains every being in its essential nature and (as we shall see) the norms of every ethical command. And it is identical with the Holy, the ground of everything that has being.

Again, all this does not deny the relativism in cognitive encounters with reality. But it shows that relativism is only possible on the basis of a structure of absolutes. These absolutes are not statements with absolute claims to truth, but they are expressions of the fact that there is a structure or a *logos* in encountered reality. Reality is structured, no matter how much it is always changing and no matter how the description of this structure may change.

Perhaps my description seems merely theoretical, and you are wondering what the moral and religious implications can be. However, you don't need to wait for a discussion of these implications. There are some among us for whom theoretical problems are existential, are matters of "to be, or not to be," because *theoria* means "looking at" things and being united with them in this way. My statements are primarily addressed to these. I myself belong to them. For us, the question of the cognitive encounter with reality, the question of the absolute and the relative in this encounter, is an existential concern—a concern that involves our whole existence. I should like it to be so for many, because ultimately knowing is an act of love.

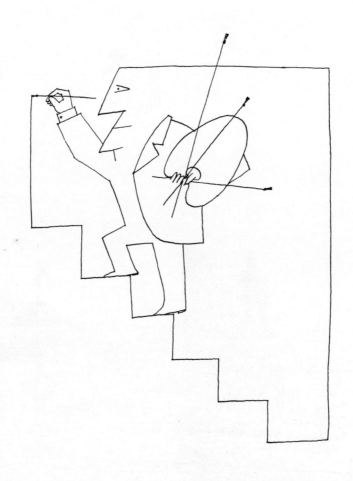

III

The Absolute and the Relative
Element in Moral Decisions

MY PREVIOUS CHAPTER FOUND and described absolutes in terms of certainty of truth: man's immediate sense impressions and the logical and semantic structure of his mind. I did not quote, in that chapter, but shall do so here, from a correspondence between the British philosopher Locke and the German philosopher Leibnitz. Locke wrote, "There is nothing in the mind which is not in the senses." Leibnitz answered, "Except the mind itself." This is just what I meant when I discussed the logical and semantic structure of our minds.

Then, in reality as encountered, we found absolutes in the concepts that make language possible, the universals; and absolutes that make understanding possible, the categories and polarities of being.

Finally, we found absolutes in what were called in the Middle Ages the *"transcendentalia,"* the good and the true and being-itself (or being as being).

The Absolute Character of the Moral Imperative

Now we have come to that encounter of man with reality which is expressed in his moral experience. The first thing I want to point to is the absolute character of the moral imperative. It means, if something is demanded of us morally, this demand is an unconditional one. The fact that the contents of the moral imperative change according to one's situation in time and space does not change the formal absoluteness of the moral imperative itself. In the moment in which we acknowledge something as our moral duty, under whatever conditions, this duty is unconditional. Whether we obey it or not is another question with which I shall deal later, but if we acknowledge it as a moral command it is unconditional and nothing should prevent us from fulfilling it.

This absoluteness was most sharply formulated by Immanuel Kant when he spoke of the "categorical imperative," another way of expressing an unconditional non-hypothetical imperative. The term indicates that it is impossible to derive a moral imperative from other sources than its own intrinsic nature. If you could derive it from fear of punishment it would be a conditional imperative, involved with social conventions, with punishments and rewards, but it would not be unconditional and absolutely serious, and you might cleverly escape the punishments.

If it were derived from calculation of what is most useful in the long or short run, as it was in some philosophical schools, it would be dependent on the cleverness of such calculation, but it would not be unconditional and absolutely serious.

If it were derived from authorities, earthly or heavenly, which were not identical with the nature of the moral imperative itself, it would not be unconditional and we should have to reject it.

To understand this we must ask about the rise of moral consciousness in past history and today, every day, for with each unique human being moral consciousness develops anew. Its source is the encounter of person with person, an encounter in which each person constitutes an absolute limit for the other. Each person, in being a person, makes the demand not to be used as a means. We can run ahead in the world in knowing and acting, in every direction, in every dimension. We can make use of all kinds of things in order to do this. But suddenly we encounter a person, a being who says without words, simply by being a person, "Just to this point and not beyond! Acknowledge me as a person. You cannot use me as a means." And we say the same thing to him. Both of us demand acknowledgment as persons. My demand on him is as unconditional as his demand on me.

That which is only a thing, or predominantly a thing, can be used. But if one uses a person one abuses not only him but also one's self, and it is this that creates the unconditional character of the moral imperative. If I use a person as a thing I myself lose my dignity as a person. This, of course, is a description of the norm, the validity of which we can experience. In reality it has always been trespassed, broken, violated; and we violate it continually. Here is the birthplace of the unconditional character of the moral imperative.

Now we ask: Why is this imperative unconditionally valid? The answer is: because it is our own true or essential being that confronts us in the moral command, demanding something from us in our actual being with all its problems and distortions. If we act against this command from our true being, we violate ourselves. If the moral command (whatever its content is) comes from any other source than our true being, if it is imposed on us from outside, if it comes from authorities of any kind, it is not an unconditional command for us. Then we can and must resist it, because it denies our own dignity as persons.

Religious ethics say that the moral command is a divine command, that it expresses "the will of God."

"The will of God" is a symbolic way of speaking, and we must interpret it in order to deprive it of connotations of arbitrariness on the part of a heavenly tyrant. God's will is given to us in the way we are created, which means it is given through our true nature, our essential being. It is not something arbitrary that falls from heaven; it is the structure of our true being that speaks to us in the moral command. If we were united with our essential being, there would be no command. We would be what we should be, and do what we should do. There would be no "ought to be," no command, "Thou shalt . . ." only simple being.

This, however, is not the case. We are separated from our true, our essential being, and therefore it stands against us, it commands and commands unconditionally. Someone may ask: "Why should I not violate myself by disobeying what my true being demands of me? Why should I not throw away my dignity as a person, even destroy myself as a person?"

This question can be answered only if we turn our thoughts toward another dimension, the dimension of the holy. From the point of view of the holy, we do not belong to ourselves but to that from which we come and to which we return—the eternal ground of everything that is. This is the ultimate reason for the sacredness of the person and, consequently, for the unconditional character of the moral

command not to destroy our essential being which
is given to us and which we may disregard and
destroy.

All this is the first and fundamental step toward
an understanding of the absolute, present in the
moral imperative. I repeat: What commands us is
our own essential nature, our unique and eternally
significant true being. It speaks to us and demands
of us that we do not waste and destroy it.

The Relativity of Moral Contents

Now we must consider the other side of the
moral imperative, the relativity of moral contents.
In contrast to the unconditional character of the
moral imperative as such, its contents are always
changing.

There are three main reasons for this. The first
and basic reason is the absolute concreteness of
every situation in which a moral decision is required. The second is changes in the temporal dimension, in the flux of time. The third is differences
in the spatial dimension, differences of place.
Groups, cultures and religions, even when united
within a single political framework, lie alongside
each other and constitute a pluralistic society.

Here I must do something that seems to counter-
act my search for absolutes. I must try to undercut
false absolutes in order to discover true ones, and
I shall do this by making the false absolutes relative.

Let us look again at each of the three reasons for
the relativity of moral contents. The first was concreteness of the situation in which we make a moral
choice. By "moral choice" I do not mean a choice
between "good" and "bad," if one knows or thinks
he knows what is "good" and what is "bad." I mean
a choice between different possibilities offering
themselves as morally good.

The normal situation is that not many choices are
given, not many decisions have to be made, and
often it is possible to avoid entirely the risks involved in choosing and deciding. To avoid them
seems to be safer, for they endanger the security
that fixed moral laws give us.

Fixed moral laws allow us to believe that we
know what is good, whether we do it or not. In this
respect, there is no insecurity. We can live safely
within moral traditions as they have been formulated in legal systems, in social conventions, or in
theological or philosophical thought. Behind them
often lie ancient sacred laws, for example, the Ten
Commandments that have authority for Judaism,
Christianity, and the whole Western world. These
traditional moral laws have become internalized by
imitation and indoctrination. They are implanted in
the depths of our being by religious or social pres-
sures, threats of punishment and offers of reward,
until they have become part of us and have created
a securely functioning conscience that reacts quickly

and feels safe without experiencing the pain of having to decide. A conscience of this kind is like an
island undisturbed by external attacks and internal
conflicts. It is static, not dynamic, monistic, not
pluralistic. The culture as a whole is accepted as the
absolute; no individual decisions are necessary.

But such an island never existed, and certainly it
is not our own reality. No moral system was ever
completely safe, and the first reason for this is the
uniqueness of every concrete situation. Laws—I
think again here of the Ten Commandments—are,
on the one hand, too abstract to cover any concrete
situation and, on the other, not abstract enough to
become general principles, but depend on the culture that produced them.

The Mosaic law—the Decalogue—forbids killing, but does not say which kind of killing is forbid-
den. Even if one translates the Hebrew word *katla*
as "murder," the question is: How is murder to be
defined as distinct from killing in general? This law
does not answer, for example, questions of juridical
and military killing, or of killing in self-defense.
What about the Commandment to honor one's parents? This law presupposes something like the fetal
situation of complete dependence. How can we apply it to our liberal democratic situation and to our
need to free ourselves from the authority of our
parents?

Theologians and lawgivers always have been

aware of this problem and have written innumerable
commentaries on the ancient laws. At the moment,
however, in which one of us comes to an absolutely
concrete situation and has to make a moral decision,
he hardly turns to a commentary for help! Commentaries could not provide real answers to actual
problems, because none of the writers of such commentaries were in the exact situation you and I are
in at this moment. A decision must be risked.

A second reason for there being no safety in any
moral system is that every concrete situation is open
to different laws. We call this "a conflict of duties,"
and it is a continuous reality in the lives of all of us.
Through discussions with medical men I have come
to see how heavy a burden for many of them is the
choice between truth and compassion toward criti-
cally ill or dying patients. To tell these patients the
truth, they feel, is cruel; not to tell it to them offends
the dignity of man. There is a conflict, and no commentary can give the answer to him who as doctor
confronts this unique person, his patient. He must
make a decision, and his decision may be wrong.

A third relativity of the moral contents is that of
the conscience. I have described the internalization
of the moral command and its creation of a quickly
responding conscience. Even this does not give
something absolute. There can be a split conscience.
A split conscience is one in which two different in-
ternalizations fight with each other, or in which our

courage to dare a new step fights with our bondage to the tradition into which we were indoctrinated.

There is also the erring conscience. We saw it in some of the Nazis who committed atrocities with good consciences because "the voice of God," for them identical with the voice of Hitler, commanded them. But no excuse of outer authorities can free us from the burden of decision in the relativities of our human situation. If we hand over to an outside authority, secular or religious, this painful freedom given to us as persons, we diminish the burden of having to decide, but we also diminish our dignity as persons.

These problems are real in any culture, but they are tremendously intensified in our own, which is so thoroughly dynamic. Of course, there are dynamics even in the oldest and most static societies. Creative individuals transform the given culture slowly and almost invisibly, and there can be sudden radical changes due, for example, to political revolutions that bring about a change of ruling groups and hence of values, and there is the impact these have on laws and social conventions. New social strata become dominant, and their ideologies are imposed on the whole of society and become more and more internalized. This means that a new conscience is created.

The same things happen when there are religious and philosophical revolutions like the Reformation,

Humanism, Naturalism and Existentialism. Older moral traditions are undercut and new ones are produced. Religious and philosophical revolutions often coincide with technical revolutions that change the external world, and such changes produce ethical and moral consequences that are hidden at first, then become visible. Even if ethical theory tries to follow these changes, life cannot wait for its results. Decisions must be made in every moment.

The relativism produced by temporal changes is intensified by increasing spatial interpenetration. If in one and the same political unity elements of different traditions stand beside each other, we have a pluralistic society like our own. Looking back into history, we find that a pluralism such as we have today in this country was nowhere possible before the seventeenth century. First, there had to be the Renaissance and its relativizing effects in culture, the Reformation and its relativizing effects in religion. Until about the year 1600 Western society was religiously monolithic, then some pluralism was accepted, but only slowly and painfully and under the impact of the most horrible of all wars, the Wars of Religion. Today we live in a definite pluralism. We all know this even if we do not speak of it theoretically, for we experience it politically, culturally, and religiously.

Now that I have described the main causes of our moral relativism, I want to discuss some of its consequences. They are far-reaching. Moral decisions are unavoidable for all of us. Every judgment made by the elder generation about the younger one must take into consideration our situation of living in a dynamic and pluralistic society. The younger generation in this period have a heavy burden to carry whenever they attempt to find the way that is morally right. It is a burden not of their own making, therefore we should not judge them too easily.

Of course, many of the younger generation as well as many of the elder one try to escape by remaining safely in the traditions that have formed them. Others avoid the moral problem by making shrewd calculations of what might be the most advantageous way to take. Sometimes this is successful, if only for a short time.

However, there are many—and I know this—who face the situation and courageously take upon themselves the burden of all the relativisms and all the alternatives. Sometimes the problem is a decision between religion and secularism in one's life and thought. Or it is a decision between a conservative and a liberal political attitude, or between national and supranational interests. It can be a decision between affirmation and denial of one's vital fulfillment, especially in relation to sex, or one between acceptance of bondage to paternal or maternal authority and a breakthrough to maturity. It can be a decision between unlimited competition in vocational or business life and a valuation of life in terms of meaning and inner fulfillment, without regard for external success. Or perhaps it is a decision between permanent self-sacrifice, resignation of a full life of one's own (a daughter's self-sacrifice for her parents, a mother's for her children), and the duty to actualize one's own potentialities.

Those who are faced with having to make such decisions and the innumerable others with which life can confront us ask with utter seriousness the question of the absolute in moral decisions. They know that the risks they take in every decision can lead them to the edge of self-destruction in many different senses of this word. Therefore they look for principles to guide them, stars to show the way over a limitless ocean of relativities. They have made one decision already—not to escape decisions —and this is the most fundamental and courageous one, if it is carried through. They have left the security of the harbor of tradition. Now they look for guiding stars.

Many of us are in this situation, although some not as radically or as consciously as others. It is the situation of day-to-day life, and it is not always dramatic. However, it often happens that through many small decisions one great decision becomes real for us even before we realize that we have already decided.

Principles of Moral Decision

Now let us look for what I have called "stars," meaning principles of moral decision that are absolutes in the relativity of ethical contents, criteria liberating us not from the necessity of deciding but from the danger of falling into willfulness and mere contingency.

The word "decision" comes from the Latin *decidere*, "to cut through, to cut off." Every decision necessarily is a cutting through something and a cutting off of other possibilities. But this means also that a decision can be willful, made arbitrarily without a guiding norm. Therefore we ask: Are there guiding principles by which we can distinguish genuine decisions from the compulsions of willfulness? If there are, they must be absolute on one side, relative on the other. An absolute principle for moral decisions has to be both. If it were not absolute it could not save us from drowning in the chaos of relativism. If it were not relative it could not enter into our relative situation, the ethical contents.

Our search for such principles can start with the absolute we spoke of earlier, the unconditional imperative to acknowledge every person as a person. If we ask for the contents given by this absolute, we find, first, something negative—the command not to treat a person as a thing. This seems little, but it is much. It is the core of the principle of justice.

Justice has many facets. For Plato, it was the most embracing virtue of all the virtues. Aristotle emphasized proportionate justice that gives to each one what he deserves. The Stoics emphasized the element of equality in justice and demanded the emancipation of women, children, strangers, and slaves.

This side of the principle of justice could lead us into problems of social ethics. There is the question whether the absolutes that appear in personal moral decisions are analogous to decisions of social groups made through their leaders. If so, such an analogy is limited, first, by the fact that a group is not centered in the way an individual is. A group is not a person, and this changes the whole ethical situation.

I'd like to say also, as a kind of footnote here, that those who for seemingly moral reasons want to push the analogy as far as possible and make the state into a person do so in order to judge the state by the same principles by which they judge individuals, including themselves. What they actually do, however, in emphasizing the analogy, is to prepare the way for dictators, for totalitarianism. This is because at the moment in which the state is thought of as a person, the leader of the state becomes its center, its deliberating and deciding center, and there is no longer a possibility of criticizing him. Therefore, I ask those who are deeply concerned about the moral problem in this respect to avoid placing an emphasis on such an analogy.

There is a second and equally important reason why the principle of justice applies differently to groups. It is the fact that centered social groups have power structures and cannot be judged in the same way as individuals. There are many moral decisions an individual has to make in his relation to centered social groups like states, and these come under our problem, but the actions of such groups in relation to other groups and to individuals lie in another dimension and demand other forms of inquiry. Justice is a principle for them also, but it is not the justice of individuals confronted by the necessity of making moral decisions.

The principle of justice, as found in the Old Testament, has the element of righteousness. This is more than formal acknowledgment of the other person and more than proportionate justice that gives to each one what he deserves. *Sedaqah* can be called "creative justice," because it does something to the other person; it changes his condition. *Sedaqah* raises to a higher state him to whom it is given. It raises the proportion of what is due him.

In the New Testament, justice has an additional element that does not deny any of the others. This element is love, in New Testament Greek *agape* (and I use the Greek word here because of the great diversity of meanings of the word "love"). *Agape* is the fulfillment of the creative justice of the Old Testament. Its highest expression is self-sacrifice for him who is loved and with whom in this way a profound union is created. Therefore *agape*-love goes far beyond the acknowledgment of the other person as a person. It wants reunion with the other and with everything from which one is separated.

Love in its character of *agape* is the absolute moral principle, the ethical absolute for which we were searching. However, to be correctly understood it must be purged of many wrong connotations. Love as *agape* has the basic principle of justice within itself. If people deny justice to others but say that they love them, they miss completely the meaning of *agape*. They combine injustice with sentimentality and call this love. *Agape* also must not be confused with other qualities of love: *libido,* friendship, compassion, pity, *eros.* Certainly *agape* is related to and can be combined with all of them, but it also judges all of them. Its greatness is that it accepts and tolerates the other person even if he is unacceptable to us and we can barely tolerate him. Its aim is a union that is more than a union on the basis of sympathy or friendship, a union even in spite of enmity. Loving one's enemies is not sentimentality; the enemy remains an enemy. In spite of this, he is not only acknowledged as a person; he is united with me in something that is above him and me, the ultimate ground of the being of each of us.

Agape is the absolute moral principle, the "star" above the chaos of relativism. However, we need more than one star to guide us. A second is the concrete situation to which love turns in a way I like to call "listening love." "Listening love" is a listening to and looking at the concrete situation in all its concreteness, which includes the deepest motives of the other person. Today we can understand the inner situation of another person better than people could in earlier periods. We have the help of psychological and sociological insights into the internal as well as the external conditions of an individual's predicament. These can be of aid to *agape* in its listening to and looking at the concrete situation.

"Listening love" takes the place of mechanical obedience to moral commandments. Such commandments were derived from ethical insights, then became degraded to the status of moral codes. No moral code, however, can spare us from a decision and thus save us from a moral risk. It can advise but can do nothing more. This becomes clear to us when we are in the position of counseling someone. Let us suppose that a student comes to me faced with a difficult moral decision. In counseling him I don't quote the Ten Commandments, or the words of Jesus in the Sermon on the Mount, or any other law, not even a law of general humanistic ethics. Instead, I tell him to find out what the commandment of *agape* in his situation is, and then decide for it even if traditions and conventions stand against his decision. However, I must add a warning as well and tell him that if he does so, he risks tragedy. Moral commandments are the wisdom of the past as it has been embodied in laws and traditions, and anyone who does not follow them risks tragedy.

This leads to a general consideration of the function of the law, the Ten Commandments, the Sermon on the Mount, the Epistles, the law of Islam, and the laws of other religions. These laws are not absolute, but they are consequences derived from the absolute principle of *agape,* love united with justice and experienced in innumerable encounters with concrete situations in human history. The lists of moral commandments, wherever they appear in history, express the moral experience of mankind. They can be called the work of Wisdom, the divine power that guided God in the creation of the world and speaks in the streets of the city. They represent the ethical wisdom of the ages, and one should not disregard them easily. Only if one recognizes the inadequacy of the law for a concrete situation can one feel justified in disobeying it.

I want to say two things about those who dare to make genuine moral decisions. In making such decisions courageously, guided by the principle of *agape,* looking with "listening love" into the concrete situation, helped by the wisdom of the ages, they do something not only for themselves and for those in relation to whom they decide. They actualize possibilities of spiritual life which had remained hidden until then; therefore they participate creatively in shaping the future ethical consciousness. This is the creative excitement of moral life, the possibility of which is given today especially to the younger generation. Certainly, it is a great burden. It has thrown them into an insecurity far exceeding the insecurity experienced by older generations, for whom the problem was: Do I do the good I know, or don't I? Of course, this remains the problem for all of us, in all times. But the new generation today must ask, in addition: What is the good? Therefore they must make decisions, and moral decisions imply moral risks. However, even though a decision may be wrong and bring suffering, the creative element in every serious choice can give the courage to decide. This was the first thing I wanted to say about those who dare to make genuine moral decisions.

Now I shall say the second thing about them. The more seriously one has considered all the factors involved in a moral decision, the absolute as well as the relative factors, the more one can be certain that there is a power of acceptance in the depth of life. It is the power by which life accepts us *in spite of* the violation of life we may have committed by making a wrong decision.

The mixture of the absolute and the relative in moral decisions is what constitutes their danger and their greatness. It gives dignity and tragedy to man, creative joy and pain of failure. Therefore he should not try to escape into a willfulness without norms, or into a security without freedom.

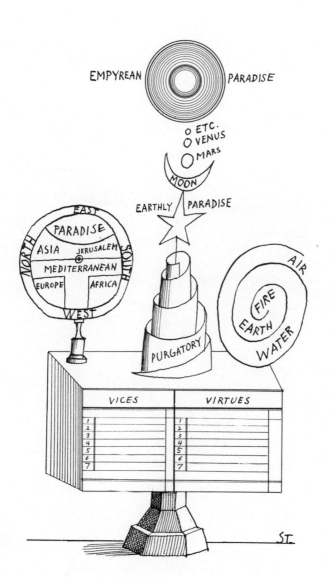

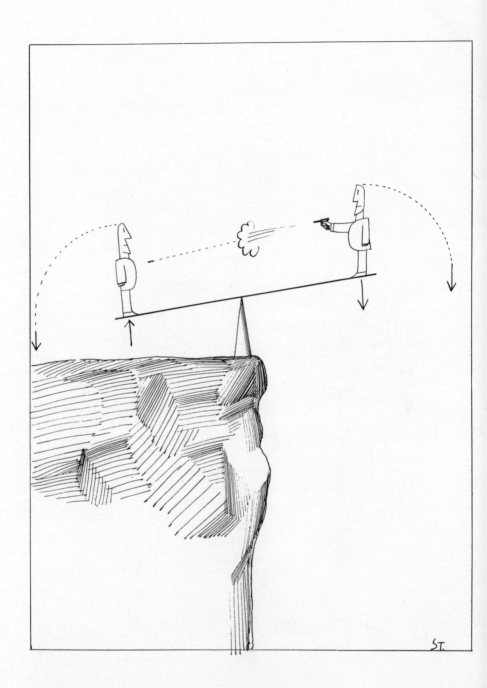

person + person = person person

person + person + person = 3

person + 3 = 4

eagle + = eagle

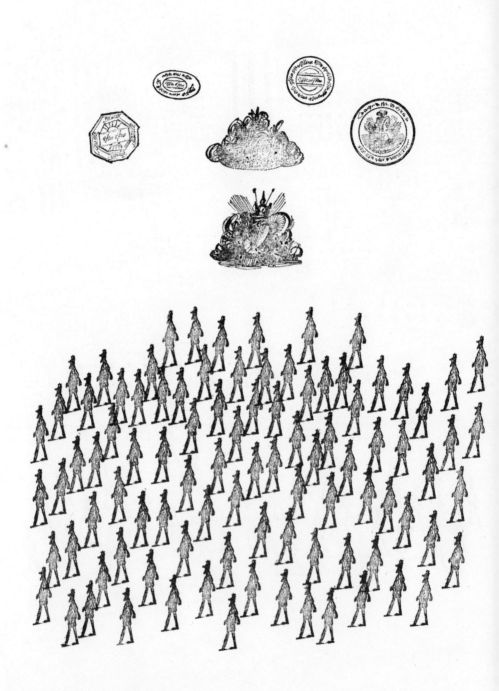

STEINBERG

IV

The Holy—the Absolute and the Relative in Religion

THE TWO PREVIOUS CHAPTERS did three different things. First, they described my concern for the relativity of man as subject and the relativity of reality as object in terms of our cognitive and moral encounters. Second, they found absolutes, the basis of my theology, on both the subjective and the objective sides, in the midst of these relativities.

These absolutes were: the structure of the mind that makes sense impressions possible, and the logical and semantic structure of the mind; the universals that make language possible; the categories and polarities that make understanding of reality possible. Others were the unconditional character of the moral imperative, regardless of its contents, and the principle of justice—acknowledgment of every person as a person. Finally, there was *agape,* love, which contains and transcends justice and unites the absolute and the relative by adapting itself to every concrete situation.

In the course of our search, however, we found something else that leads to the problem I shall deal with now. We found that all the absolutes pointed beyond themselves to the most basic absolute of all, to being-itself beyond the split of subject and object.

In finding being-itself, our search has reached the ground of truth and of the good, the source of all the other absolutes in our encounter with reality. This source is the Absolute-itself, and the experience of the Absolute-itself is experience of the holy, the sacred.

We could also have reached this source of all absolutes from an analysis of other kinds of encounter with reality—for instance, the aesthetic encounter. It would seem that relativism is completely dominant in the realm of aesthetics. People often say that aesthetic tastes cannot be discussed; nevertheless, one can discuss whether a contemporary painting or a sculpture of 2000 B.C., can be called a work of art. There are certainly some absolutes for judging art, as long as one distinguishes art from other functions such as technology, science, and so on, and the great work of art has in itself something absolute, insofar as it expresses ultimate reality. It does this by being a piece of finite reality through which, thanks to the artist's creative power, ultimate reality shines and gives it inexhaustible meaning. This pointing beyond itself of every work of art shows the presence of something absolute in art, despite all changing styles and tastes in the realm of artistic creation.

There is another realm that could be treated separately, the social-political. In the social-political realm it is particularly the *sacredness* of the law that is expressed in many ways in most law systems, and this feeling for the sacredness of the law has survived the attack of secularism. We can recognize it in the form of oaths and in the quasi-ritualistic attitudes of the law court where contempt of court could be described as secularized blasphemy. We can recognize it in the awe felt toward this country's "law of the land," especially toward its social-political foundation, the Constitution. We can recognize it in the mythological "will of the people" and "tradition of the fathers" and in the equally mythological emperor or king "by the grace of God." Laws and constitutions change, but their legal and social validity is absolute. This is because they are rooted in the holy itself.

The way to the Absolute as such, the ground of every absolute in a particular realm, is anagogical (from the Greek word meaning "leading upward"). In showing the way to the Absolute itself, we did not start from ultimate reality, nor did we argue for the existence of God, but we tried to show that within the different realms of man's encounter with reality —the cognitive, the ethical, and (barely under the wire) the aesthetic and the social-political—he finds structural absolutes without which life in these realms would be impossible. Going beyond this, we tried to show that in each of these structural absolutes there is a point of self-transcendence toward the Absolute itself, the ground of being experienced as the holy. In the cognitive encounter this point of self-transcendence is being-itself; in the ethical encounter it is love in its character of *agape,* which contains justice and combines the absolute and the relative. In other words, we have shown by analytic description the presence of absolutes within the universe of relativities and have pointed to the ground of everything absolute—the Absolute itself. The method we have followed liberates us from thinking in terms of questions and arguments about the existence of an absolute being, whether it is called "God," or the One, or Brahman-Atman, Fate, Nature, or Life. That to which our analysis led us, the Absolute itself, is not an absolute being, which is a contradiction in terms. It is Being-Itself.

Man's Encounter with the Holy

The encounter of man with ultimate reality, which we call the encounter with the holy, in its essence is not an encounter beside other encounters. It is within the others. It is the experience of the Absolute, of absoluteness as such. Only after this statement has been made can one speak of a particular encounter with the holy—that is, of "religion" in the traditional sense of the word. In the encounter with the holy an experience of the Absolute as such is not only implied but intended, and this is decisive for the meaning of religion. It is this intention to encounter the Absolute as such which makes religion religion and at the same time transcends religion infinitely.

The religious absolute is most sharply expressed in the Great Commandment: "You shall love the Lord your God with all your heart, and with all your soul, and with all your mind, and with all your strength." This is absoluteness in religious language, and it is the basis of my definition of religion as "the state of being grasped by an ultimate concern." The Great Commandment is Jewish and Christian, but there are similar expressions of absoluteness in all religions.

An absolute threat and an absolute promise are present in many religions, symbolized, for instance, in the images of hell and heaven which can be understood psychologically as ultimate despair and highest blessedness. These symbols cut into the relativities of ordinary pleasure and pain, joy and sorrow, hope and doubt. They express two absolute possibilities that depend on the relation to the Ultimate itself. We have strong expressions of them in

Islam, Hinduism, Mahayana Buddhism, and, certainly, in Christianity and Judaism. What is really symbolized in "hell" and "heaven" is the absolute seriousness of the relation to the Holy, to the Absolute itself.

This agrees with Rudolph Otto's analysis of "the idea of the holy." When I use this phrase, "the idea of the holy," I remember wonderful hours in Marburg, Germany, in the mid-Twenties, when Rudolph Otto and I walked together through the hills and woods and talked about the problems of Christianity and the Asiatic religions (of which he was a great scholar and to which he returned again and again). The first thing he said in his analysis of the meaning of the term "holy" was that "the holy" is "mystery" and means the Absolute itself, the ground of all the absolutes we have discovered in the different realms of man's encounter with reality. It cannot be derived from our finite experience, nor can it be grasped in its essence by finite minds at all. Nevertheless, we can be related to and know we are related to that which is mystery to us and to every human being, a mystery of man's own being in universal being. In experiencing this mystery, man is driven to ask the question: "Why is there something and not nothing?"

Otto expresses the relation of our mind to the Ultimate and its mystery in two terms: *"tremendum"* —that which produces trembling, fear, and awe;

and *"fascinosum"*—that which produces fascination, attraction, and desire. Man's unconditional awe of and unconditional attraction to the holy are what he means in these two terms, and they imply the threat of missing one's possible fulfillment. The dread of missing one's fulfillment—this is the awe. The desire to reach one's fulfillment—this is the attraction.

Otto makes use of examples from all religions and shows that these examples all point to one thing: In these experiences people have encountered the Absolute as absolute above all derived absolutes in the different realms.

The Two Concepts of Religion

Now a question arises that is decisive for our whole cultural situation today. Is the encounter with the Absolute-itself restricted to experiences within what traditionally is called "religion"?

My answer is: Certainly not. I have already discovered and described absolutes outside religion in my two previous chapters. Here I can say that something is holy to everyone, even to those who deny that they have experienced the holy.

This leads us to distinguish two concepts of religion, a larger concept and a narrower one, and the different ways in which the Absolute is experienced in them. The larger concept of religion has appeared as the dimension of ultimate reality in the different realms of man's encounter with reality. It is, to use a metaphor, the dimension of depth itself, the inexhaustible depth of being, but it appeared indirectly in these realms. What was experienced directly was knowledge, or the moral imperative, or social justice, or aesthetic expressiveness; but the holy was present in all these secular structures, although hidden in them. For this is how one experiences the holy, through secular structures. Religion in this basic and universal sense I have called "being grasped by an ultimate concern."

This definition, however, is also valid for the narrower concept of religion. The difference is that here the experience of the Ultimate is direct. I have usually described it as the experience of the holy in a particular presence, place, or time, in a particular person, book, or image, in a particular ritual act, spoken word, or sacramental object. These direct experiences are found in unity with a sacred community, in the Western world usually called a church, a monastic group, or a religious movement. Such a community expresses the particular character of its experience of the holy in its special symbols of imagination and cult and in special rules that determine its ethical and social life. This is religion in the narrower, the traditional sense.

The relation of the two concepts is obvious. The first, the larger one, represents the Absolute beyond religion and non-religion. The second, the narrower

one, represents the Absolute in a direct concrete sym-
bolization. This relationship has many consequences
for human existence, of which the most important
is that the Absolute, the Holy-itself, transcends and
judges every religion. The ultimate in being and
meaning cannot be limited, cannot be caught in any
particular religion, in any particular sacred place or
by any particular sacred action.

But even this statement, that God cannot be
caught in any particular religion, could have been
made only on the basis of a particular religion, a
religion able to transcend its own particularity and,
because it can do this, having perhaps a critical
power in relation to other religions.

In any case, the larger concept of religion is the
basis of the narrower concept and judges those religions described by the narrower concept. This in-
sight has important consequences, both for the
relation of religions to one another and for their relation to the secular realm. It gives, among other
things, a positive religious meaning to secularism,
which usually is condemned in sermons and publi-
cations of the church.

Demonization of Religion

There is a phenomenon we could call "the demonization of religion." When we speak of "the
demonic" we mean more than failure and distortion, more than intentional evil. The demonic is a

negative absolute. It is the elevation of something relative and ambiguous (something in which the negative and the positive are united) to absoluteness. The ambiguous, in which positive and negative, creative and destructive elements are mingled, is considered sacred in itself, is deified. In the case of religion, the deification of the relative and the ambiguous means that a particular religion claims to be identical with the religious Absolute and rejects judgment against itself. This leads, internally, to demonic suppression of doubt, criticism, and honest search for truth within the particular religion itself; and it leads, externally, to the most demonic and destructive of all wars, religious wars. Such evils are unavoidable if a particular manifestation of the holy is identified with the holy itself.

Conspicuous examples of demonization of religion are the Inquisition (internal) and the Thirty Years' War (external). But many similar events can be found in the histories of all religions.

The immediate consequence of the Thirty Years' War was the most powerful development of secularization in all history, beginning with the secular state that took control in order to save Europe from complete self-destruction. At the same time, a secularized philosophy and the relativizing tendency that went with scientific progress undercut the struggling churches' claims to absoluteness. Secularism in this sense can be considered a judgment by the true Absolute of demonic claims to absoluteness made by particular religions or by groups within a particular religion.

The Quasi-Religions

The process of secular relativization has now reached an almost unsurpassable stage in both theory and practice, as I ʼdmitted in Chapter Two. However, this stage in which we find ourselves today has produced a counter-movement, a movement toward new absolutes on the basis of secularism. We find these absolutes in the quasi-religions and their consequences, quasi-religious wars (one of which we are living through today).

Anyone who has seen, as I have, the rush toward new absolutes in the period of the rise of Fascism, Nazism, and Communism, especially by the younger generation of that time, has understood the quasi-religious character of these movements. Like traditional religions, they elevate their basic dogmas beyond question and make them refer to all areas of man's life. Ethical decisions are determined by commandments imposed externally at first, then (and this is more dangerous) internalized in the consciences of the people. These commandments are also internalized in the legal and social structures which now depend on the implications of the basic dogma, in the ritual forms which sanction the whole, and in the artistic expressions which are now means to propagate the system's truth and glory. The result is systems of life with an all-pervasive absolute, under an authority that is absolute, and generating absolutes in all parts of themselves. We live among such systems today.

Besides Fascism (Nazism) and Communism there is a third political-cultural system, the so-called "West," meaning, particularly, the Anglo-Saxon nations and, even more particularly, ourselves. It is a system quasi-religious in nature, and it can be called "liberal humanism."

This system has fought in the name of its absolutes, liberalism and humanism, against the other two absolutes, Fascism and Communism. It has conquered the first, at least so far, and continues to oppose the other. The superiority of our system is its attempt to find a way that bypasses, on the one hand, the self-negating absolute of relativism and, on the other, the demonized absolutes of Fascism and Communism. However, let us not have any doubt about ourselves. Ours is a quasi-religious system also. Its absolute is most impressively embodied in the Constitution, which permeates all areas of our lives. A delicate balance has been achieved between this basic absolute and an almost limitless relativity; but we should recognize that this balance is always threatened. In its struggles against the other absolutes, liberal humanism can easily model itself on its adversaries. It, too, can suppress—by indirect means—liberal criticism coming from its own citizens. From outside, it can be maneuvered into a position in which it has to defend humanism by means that by their very nature are inhuman. Liberal humanism can sacrifice, out of tragic necessity, its liberalism internally and its humanism externally. Or, in the hope of avoiding these consequences, it can surrender its own absolutes and fall into complete theoretical and practical relativism.

A serious struggle is going on today in this country against the menace of cultural and moral disintegration. It is a struggle made difficult for believers in liberal humanism by those who participate in it with them but do not believe in liberal humanism and use the struggle to build up a new nationalistic absolutism similar to the one the United States fought against in the name of freedom and humanity. Such undesirable allies drive believers in liberal humanism the other way into extremes of relativism. (I should like to think that here I have described a problem that concerns you as much as it concerns me but is of even greater import to the younger generation, whose destiny is decided in these conflicts.)

The Question of a Particular Religion's Claim to Universal Absoluteness

After this seeming excursus to the quasi-religions (which should not be called "pseudo-religions," because there is much genuine passion, commitment, and faith in them), I want finally to discuss a question I know is in the minds of many people today.

If the Absolute-itself, the ground of all absolutes, is manifest in particular religions, is there perhaps one religion which can claim absoluteness for itself above all the others?

Obviously, most of the great religions have made this universal claim, and some still do so, notably Christianity, Islam, and their common origin, Judaism. There are others that do not claim absoluteness universally, but only for a special limited culture. I call them the pets of the cultural anthropologists, who are always happy when they can identify religion with a culture—for example, the culture of some Pacific island aborigines—and thus remove its seriousness. This group, however, includes some great religions that have never become missionary: Shintoism in Japan, Hinduism in India, and Confucianism in China. These religions make no claims to universal absoluteness; rather, they claim validity for their special forms of culture. They are examples of the phenomenon of a particular absolute that accepts its particularity and doesn't go beyond it.

Over against both groups is a religion that is important here in a negative sense, Buddhism. Buddhism in its original form rejected divine figures. Later it did not reject them, and it now accepts many Bodhisattvas as representatives of the Bud-

dha-spirit and can accept also, as Buddhists often
tell us, Moses, Jesus, and Mohammed. This seems
to be self-relativization of a radical kind, but it is
not. Buddhism's acceptance of these figures is possible only because when they are taken into Buddhism they no longer have the meaning they had in
their original setting. In their original setting they
were concrete representatives of the positive and exclusive Absolute, not merely relative manifestations of the same spirit that was in the Buddha and
can return innumerable times in different figures.

This means that the decisive problem is posed by
those religions each of which claims absoluteness
for a particular revelatory experience: Judaism,
Christianity, and Islam. (There are other sectarian
movements in other religions, but they have different origins and make no universal claims; and there
is a synthetic religion, Bahaism, which claims to be
all-inclusive because it puts elements of all religions
together without a new fundamental principle.)

The three great Israel-born religions are the ones
which pose the decisive problem of a universal claim
to absoluteness on the part of a particular religion.
This is because of the prophetic struggle against
idolatry carried on by the prophets of Israel. Here
we can see the problem of absolutes in a new way.
Exclusive monotheism, as we find it in the Old
Testament, is by its very nature absolutistic. It had
to be exclusive because it had to fight tremendous

battles against a demonic idolatric elevation of finite objects to divinity. Sometimes these finite objects were representatives of a finite realm, who became gods; or they were gods who represented particular countries; or they were elements, like water and air; or they were social groups and nations; or particular functions of the human spirit; or they were human virtues, like wisdom, power, and justice.

Against all such idolatrous consecrations of particular realms as divine beings the prophets of Israel waged their tremendous fight to uphold the absoluteness of the Absolute. Never dismiss the problem of monotheism and idolatry as if it were a mere matter of numbers. Monotheism does not mean that one god is better than many; it means that the one is the Absolute, the Unconditional, the Ultimate. It was for this absolute, unconditional, ultimate one that the anti-idolatric struggle was carried on.

Through this struggle, somewhere in world history the absoluteness of the Absolute was established. The particular absolutes—truth, justice, and so on—became attributes of the one Absolute, the Divine. Here is the source of the universality of truth and justice and of the idea that God rejects even his own elect nation if that nation exercises injustice. I maintain that this unique conception—the rejection of that nation which represents the absoluteness of the Absolute, by the Absolute itself—is the greatest inner religious manifestation of the Absolute;

and that therefore there is no Bible without the Old Testament and the struggle of the prophets.

From this follows the inner-religious struggle of the Absolute with the relative element which claims absoluteness for itself, or (in religious language) the struggle of God against religion. In every man there is a tendency toward idolatry; in every religion, a stronger one. The disciples' attempt to use Jesus idolatrically, and Jesus' rejection of this attempt, is one of the main themes of the gospel stories. Jesus rejected the temptation to let himself be idolized; and this gives Christianity, in principle, the position of criterion not only against itself, but against all other religions. Christianity should not deny the others' validity by calling them "false religions," but in the encounter with them should drive them to the point of their own self-judgment.

Every religion has a depth that is forever covered, as it is in Christianity, by that religion's particularity. In most religions a fight has gone on, and is going on now, against distortion of the Absolute by the particular religion. The great mystical systems of the East resulted from this fight. The struggle, however, has not been radical enough anywhere for a complete liberation from distortion. Therefore in our dialogues with other religions we must not try to make converts; rather, we must try to drive the other religions to their own depths, to that point at which they realize that they are witness to the Absolute but are not the Absolute themselves.

From this realization follows, first, the statement that a particular religion's claim to absoluteness can only be a claim to witness in a relative way to the Absolute. A religion is the more true the more it implies this in its essential nature, in which it points beyond itself to that for which it is a witness and of which it is a partial manifestation.

Second, the relationship of religions to one another cannot consist primarily of desire for conversions but must consist of desire for an exchange, a mutual receiving and giving at the same time. A transition from one religion to another may result from such dialogues, but this is not their aim. The aim in these encounters is to break through mutually to that point at which the vision of the holy-itself liberates us from bondage to any of the particular manifestations of the holy.

Third, the relation of religion to the secular world, to secularism, must be changed from both sides, from the secular as well as from the religious side. Religion must affirm the right of all functions of the human spirit—the arts and sciences, the law and social relations and the state beyond them—to be independent of religious control or interference. At the same time, the secular world must affirm the right of religion to turn toward the Ultimate-itself in its language and in all its expressions of the experience of the holy.

Man's Search for an Ultimate Meaning

In this volume in Credo Perspectives I have expressed certain things that are going on in all of us in this period of history. I have spoken about the sea of relativities that threatens to overwhelm us and about man's desire to find absolutes to guide him.

This desire was so ardent in the younger generation in the first half of our century that when they found leaders who gave them absolutes they followed them, even though the absolutes were demonic ones.

The struggle for the absolute in a secularized world is an inner process in the secular realms. It is not imposed by religious aspirations but is man's reaction against being without a structure of meaning. The religions of the world must acknowledge this struggle and not destroy it by an arrogant dogmatism. They must open themselves to those who ask the question of the absolute with passion and unconditional seriousness, both inside and outside the churches.

If no human being can live without something he takes with unconditional seriousness in whatever language he expresses it, then we in our liberal humanist culture should look for this. We should look for it without the fanatical and desperate drive which in Europe led to the destruction of much of that continent; we should look for it as long as time is given to us, in a unity of theoretical understanding and practical actualization; and we should look for it in awareness that we ourselves need, far more than we have now, an ultimate meaning in our daily lives.